GAY AND LESBIAN FAMILIES

Other books in the At Issue series:

GAY AND LESBIAN FAMILIES

Kate Burns, *Book Editor*

Bruce Glassman, *Vice President*
Bonnie Szumski, *Publisher*
Helen Cothran, *Managing Editor*

GREENHAVEN PRESS
An imprint of Thomson Gale, a part of The Thomson Corporation

Detroit • New York • San Francisco • San Diego • New Haven, Conn.
Waterville, Maine • London • Munich

LIBRARY OF CONGRESS CATALOGING-IN-PUBLICATION DATA

Gay and lesbian families / Kate Burns, book editor.
    p. cm. — (At issue)
Includes bibliographical references and index.
ISBN 0-7377-2374-2 (lib. : alk. paper) — ISBN 0-7377-2375-0 (pbk. : alk. paper)
    1. Same-sex marriage—United States. 2. Same-sex marriage—Canada. 3. Gay male couples—Family relationships. 4. Lesbian couples—Family relationships. 5. Gay adoption. 6. Gay parents—Family relationships. 7. Gay teenagers—Family relationships. I. Burns, Kate, 1969– . II. At issue (San Diego, Calif.)
HQ76.35.U6G39 2005
306.85'086'64—dc22   2004047471

Printed in the United States of America

Contents

Introduction

At first glance, questions such as "what is a family?" and "what is marriage?" may seem frivolous and their answers obvious. A closer look at gay history reveals that such questions have been at the center of social, political, and religious controversies for years. Indeed, debates about gay and lesbian families illustrate the old adage, "words matter."

Scientists distinguish human beings from other species in part by their ability to communicate with spoken and written language. Words cannot be understood without common definitions that clearly convey meaning; words make things and concepts tangible. Definitions provide boundary lines that separate one idea from another in order to make them distinct—they categorize what is real and understandable. The way a word like *family* is defined can affect social policies and practices in a community. Being included in the definition often conveys important rights and privileges while being excluded bars people from these advantages. Clearly, much is at stake in the meaning of words that classify and identify people.

Those discussing gay and lesbian families often struggle over the definition of words and concepts. Activists who want equal rights for gay and lesbian parents, for example, work to expand legal and social definitions of "family" to include their partnerships and parenting roles. Those who oppose equal rights for gay and lesbian parents work to limit legal and social definitions to heterosexual couples and parents. One of the most contentious controversies in the United States today is over whether to include gays and lesbians in legal definitions of marriage. House representative Marilyn Musgrave feels so strongly about the issue that on May 21, 2003, she proposed an amendment to the U.S. Constitution that would ban same-sex marriages. Her Federal Marriage Amendment (H.J. Resolution 56) states:

> Marriage in the United States shall consist only of the union of a man and a woman. Neither this Constitution or the constitution of any State, nor state or federal law, shall be construed to require that marital status or the legal incidents thereof be conferred upon unmarried couples or groups.

Opponents of the Federal Marriage Amendment argue that the definition would destroy the spirit of the Constitution by restricting the rights of a whole group of U.S. citizens. According to the Human Rights Campaign (HRC), a national gay and lesbian rights organization:

> This amendment not only attempts to deny equal rights to gays and lesbians, but it also attempts to undermine legislative and legal efforts to protect American families who are gay and lesbian couples and their children. . . . Marriage,

7

other forms of relationship recognition, and basic civil rights protections are essential components that make all families, including families headed by same-sex couples, safer and more secure.

The battle over what to call gay relationships is the continuation of a long struggle by gays and lesbians for validation through language. The tremendous social and political pressure to hide attraction to the same sex that existed until recent years inspired nineteenth-century Irish poet Oscar Wilde to define homosexuality as "the love that dare not speak its name." While terms were used in the mainstream public to define same-sex relationships, they were most often disparaging. Public discovery of same-sex love could exact serious penalties, as it did for Wilde when he was sentenced to two years of hard labor for the crime of "sodomy" in 1895.

After Wilde's time, early generations of gay and lesbian "sexologists," who studied human sexuality, worked to reverse the stigma associated with being homosexual. Pioneers in uniting activism and scholarship, they toiled to gain more respect for gay people and protect their human rights. However, their work was repressed from 1900 to 1930. According to professors Bonnie Zimmerman and George E. Haggerty,

> Economic crisis and political repression in the United States and Europe would drive nascent gay and lesbian communities, with their potential for scholarly research and creative activity, underground. Although individuals produced monumental work, in general academic institutions generally avoided and suppressed gay and lesbian scholarship.

It was not until homophile organizations of the 1950s (the gay Mattachine Society and the lesbian Daughters of Bilitis), the women's liberation movement (including lesbian feminists), and the gay liberation movement that gays and lesbians gained considerable ground toward influencing the legal and social definitions that affected their lives. The subsequent emergence of more open gay and lesbian communities and scholarship initiated renewed study of gay and lesbian history and provided a proliferation of information about gay and lesbian life. As Zimmerman and Haggerty put it, gay and lesbian studies are the products "of an age in which self-definition is challenged by cultural urgency of various kinds and when lesbian and gay concerns have moved out from the shadows into the bright light of national and international politics." By the beginning of the twenty-first century, "the love that dare not speak its name" was being pronounced everywhere in the United States. However, far from ending struggles over words, the fight for gay and lesbian rights continues to generate additional controversies related to vocabulary and definitions.

One important debate focuses on the very terms used to represent nonheterosexual people. Just as racial minority groups have rejected pejorative words and asserted their preference for affirmative words to describe their communities, gays and lesbians have deliberated over terms such as *homosexual, gay, lesbian,* and *queer.* The word *homosexual* was first used by European and American scientists and medical doctors at the end of the nineteenth century to describe "inversion," or a person born into one gender who wishes to be the opposite gender. Same-sex attraction was considered a tragic consequence of gender confusion. Historian Gary Lehring explains:

> This understanding of homosexuality as a medical disorder entered official government discourse in the United States early in the twentieth century as a disqualification for military service, and later from all employment with the federal government. It was this repressive history that led many gay liberationists in the second half of the twentieth century to reject the term as one that had been defined and regulated by "experts."

Many gays and lesbians began to use *gay* as a preferred term. "By the 1970s," Lehring explains, "['gay'] had replaced 'homosexual' in common usage, even by heterosexuals."

At the same time, the women's liberation movement initiated a critique of masculine nouns and pronouns used to represent all people. Words such as *chairman* and *mankind* were replaced with "chairperson" and "humankind" to make them more inclusive. Women rejected what they called sexist language, and lesbians questioned whether the term *gay* similarly erased or diminished their visibility. Many in the lesbian-feminist movement of the 1970s argued that both "homosexual" and "gay" primarily referred to men, and "lesbian" should be used to designate women.

By the 1990s, another debate over language surfaced when a new generation of gay and lesbian activists and scholars began to use the term *queer* to define themselves. The trend was particularly contentious because the word had negative connotations for some older gays and lesbians who had been branded "queer" in earlier decades. Yet political organizations like Queer Nation insisted that the word be reclaimed and used instead of "gay and lesbian." Different factions had different reasons for using the term. Some found the word's second definition—"queer" as strange or disorienting—to be useful. In this sense, "queer" was used to define a political strategy of disrupting anything thought to be "normal." Queer theorists believe that no person can *be* normal, because conceptions about *normal* and *abnormal* are socially constructed by human beings, not dictated by nature or God. Others simply preferred using "queer" as a multicultural umbrella term. As writer Akila Monifa explains, "The term 'queer' was adopted for its inclusiveness, since it purports to incorporate lesbians, gay men, bisexuals, transgender people, and heterosexual allies."

Words and definitions have an impact well beyond the broad historical trends and political movements described above. On a personal level, many gays and lesbians and their families struggle to find words to define their relationships; finding the right ones, they feel, can make the difference between being accepted or rejected by others. In her essay, "When Language Fails Our Families," Abigail Garner describes the complications involved in speaking about her family relationships. As the daughter of man who was once married to a woman but who later partnered with another man, she has no exact words to accurately describe her relationship to her father's partner. She writes:

This challenge of language is not exclusive to children with partnered [gay, lesbian, bisexual, and transgendered] parents, but for almost all relationships within GLBT families. We often lack appropriate nouns, which results in the need for something close to a short paragraph to explain our relationship with each family member. . . . A mother of a gay son might confuse outsiders if she talks about her son's partner as her son-in-law. . . . I have heard people experiment with expressions like "sort of my step-sister" and "kind-of my mom" but having to put a devaluing expression like kind-of or sort-of before something as important as family rarely sits right.

Another common quandary is naming same-sex partners. Some gays and lesbians adopt common heterosexual words for their own purposes and call each other "husband" and "wife." They feel that using these terms brings them social validation. Others strongly oppose what they see as imitating a culture that excludes them. They are more likely to refer to a "significant other," "life partner," "longtime companion," or "lover." Now that gay marriage has been sanctioned in court decisions in Canada and Massachusetts, subsequent changes in the language used to describe gay and lesbian couples will likely occur.

Debates about definitions weave in and out of the selections in *At Issue: Gay and Lesbian Families*. This collection presents a diverse sampling of viewpoints about parenting, adoption, family structure, and marriage. The essays in this volume shed light on heated struggles about public policy, government intervention, civil rights, religious power, and moral principles. As the status of gay and lesbian families changes, so too will the language used to define them, for better or ill.

1

Gay Marriage Threatens Families

Stanley Kurtz

Stanley Kurtz is a research fellow at the Hoover Institution and a contributing editor at National Review Online.

Legalizing gay marriage would have a negative effect on the concept of monogamy in marriage. Homosexual activists argue that access to marriage will encourage gays and lesbians to conform to traditional monogamy in committed relationships. It is more likely that opening marriage to homosexuals will allow them to legitimize nonmonogamy, civil partnerships unrelated to sexual or romantic relationships, and polyamory (sexual relationships among more than two people). Without monogamy as a founding principle, marriage will no longer provide a stable and healthy setting for families—and especially children—to thrive. If gay marriage is legalized, the institution of marriage will be robbed of monogamy and thus any hope of permanence.

After gay marriage, what will become of marriage itself? Will same-sex matrimony extend marriage's stabilizing effects to homosexuals? Will gay marriage undermine family life? A lot is riding on the answers to these questions. But the media's reflexive labeling of doubts about gay marriage as homophobia has made it almost impossible to debate the social effects of this reform. Now with the Supreme Court's ringing affirmation of sexual liberty in *Lawrence v. Texas*, that debate is unavoidable.

Among the likeliest effects of gay marriage is to take us down a slippery slope to legalized polygamy and "polyamory" (group marriage). Marriage will be transformed into a variety of relationship contracts, linking two, three, or more individuals (however weakly and temporarily) in every conceivable combination of male and female. A scare scenario? Hardly. The bottom of this slope is visible from where we stand. Advocacy of legalized polygamy is growing. A network of grass-roots organizations seeking legal recognition for group marriage already exists. The cause of legalized group marriage is championed by a powerful faction of family law specialists. Influential legal bodies in both the United States and

Canada have presented radical programs of marital reform. Some of these quasi-governmental proposals go so far as to suggest the abolition of marriage. The ideas behind this movement have already achieved surprising influence with a prominent American politician.

None of this is well known. Both the media and public spokesmen for the gay marriage movement treat the issue as an unproblematic advance for civil rights. True, a small number of relatively conservative gay spokesmen do consider the social effects of gay matrimony, insisting that they will be beneficent, that homosexual unions will become more stable. Yet another faction of gay rights advocates actually favors gay marriage as a step toward the abolition of marriage itself. This group agrees that there is a slippery slope, and wants to hasten the slide down.

To consider what comes after gay marriage is not to say that gay marriage itself poses no danger to the institution of marriage. Quite apart from the likelihood that it will usher in legalized polygamy and polyamory, gay marriage will almost certainly weaken the belief that monogamy lies at the heart of marriage. But to see why this is so, we will first need to reconnoiter the slippery slope.

Promoting polygamy

During the 1996 congressional debate on the Defense of Marriage Act, which affirmed the ability of the states and the federal government to withhold recognition from same-sex marriages, gay marriage advocates were put on the defensive by the polygamy question. If gays had a right to marry, why not polygamists? Andrew Sullivan, one of gay marriage's most intelligent defenders, labeled the question fear-mongering—akin to the discredited belief that interracial marriage would lead to birth defects. "To the best of my knowledge," said Sullivan, "there is no polygamists' rights organization poised to exploit same-sex marriage and return the republic to polygamous abandon." Actually, there are now many such organizations. And their strategy—even their existence—owes much to the movement for gay marriage.

> *"Talking to Utah's polygamists is like talking to gays and lesbians who really want the right to live their lives."*

Scoffing at the polygamy prospect as ludicrous has been the strategy of choice for gay marriage advocates. In 2000, following Vermont's enactment of civil unions, Matt Coles, director of the American Civil Liberties Union's Lesbian and Gay Rights Project, said, "I think the idea that there is some kind of slippery slope [to polygamy or group marriage] is silly." As proof, Coles said that America had legalized interracial marriage, while also forcing Utah to ban polygamy before admission to the union. That dichotomy, said Coles, shows that Americans are capable of distinguishing between better and worse proposals for reforming marriage.

Are we? When Tom Green was put on trial in Utah for polygamy in 2001, it played like a dress rehearsal for the coming movement to legalize polygamy. True, Green was convicted for violating what he called Utah's "don't ask, don't tell" policy on polygamy. Pointedly refusing to "hide in the closet," he touted polygamy on the Sally Jessy Raphael, Queen Latifah, Geraldo Rivera, and Jerry Springer shows, and on "Dateline NBC" and "48 Hours." But the Green trial was not just a cable spectacle. It brought out a surprising number of mainstream defenses of polygamy. And most of the defenders went to bat for polygamy by drawing direct comparisons to gay marriage.

Unlike classic polygamy, which features one man and several women, polyamory comprises a bewildering variety of sexual combinations.

Writing in the *Village Voice*, gay leftist Richard Goldstein equated the drive for state-sanctioned polygamy with the movement for gay marriage. The political reluctance of gays to embrace polygamists was understandable, said Goldstein, "but our fates are entwined in fundamental ways." Libertarian Jacob Sullum defended polygamy, along with all other consensual domestic arrangements, in the *Washington Times*. Syndicated liberal columnist Ellen Goodman took up the cause of polygamy with a direct comparison to gay marriage. Steve Chapman, a member of the *Chicago Tribune* editorial board, defended polygamy in the *Tribune* and in *Slate*. The *New York Times* published a Week in Review article juxtaposing photos of Tom Green's family with sociobiological arguments about the naturalness of polygamy and promiscuity.

The ACLU's Matt Coles may have derided the idea of a slippery slope from gay marriage to polygamy, but the ACLU itself stepped in to help Tom Green during his trial and declared its support for the repeal of all "laws prohibiting or penalizing the practice of plural marriage." There is of course a difference between repealing such laws and formal state recognition of polygamous marriages. Neither the ACLU nor, say, Ellen Goodman has directly advocated formal state recognition. Yet they give us no reason to suppose that, when the time is ripe, they will not do so. Stephen Clark, the legal director of the Utah ACLU, has said, "Talking to Utah's polygamists is like talking to gays and lesbians who really want the right to live their lives."

All this was in 2001, well before the prospect that legal gay marriage might create the cultural conditions for state-sanctioned polygamy. Can anyone doubt that greater public support will be forthcoming once gay marriage has become a reality? Surely the ACLU will lead the charge.

The end of monogamy

Why is state-sanctioned polygamy a problem? The deep reason is that it erodes the ethos of monogamous marriage. Despite the divorce revolution, Americans still take it for granted that marriage means monogamy. The ideal of fidelity may be breached in practice, yet adultery is clearly understood as a transgression against marriage. Legal polygamy would jeopardize that understanding, and that is why polygamy has historically been treated in the West as an offense against society itself.

In most non-Western cultures, marriage is not a union of freely choosing individuals, but an alliance of family groups. The emotional relationship between husband and wife is attenuated and subordinated to the economic and political interests of extended kin. But in our world of freely choosing individuals, extended families fall away, and love and companionship are the only surviving principles on which families can be built. From Thomas Aquinas through Richard Posner, almost every serious observer has granted the incompatibility between polygamy and Western companionate marriage.

Where polygamy works, it does so because the husband and his wives are emotionally distant. Even then, jealousy is a constant danger, averted only by strict rules of seniority or parity in the husband's economic support of his wives. Polygamy is more about those resources than about sex.

Yet in many polygamous societies, even though only 10 or 15 percent of men may actually have multiple wives, there is a widely held belief that men need multiple women. The result is that polygamists are often promiscuous—just not with their own wives. Anthropologist Philip Kilbride reports a Nigerian survey in which, among urban male polygamists, 44 percent said their most recent sexual partners were women other than their wives. For monogamous, married Nigerian men in urban areas, that figure rose to 67 percent. Even though polygamous marriage is less about sex than security, societies that permit polygamy tend to reject the idea of marital fidelity—for everyone, polygamists included.

Mormon polygamy has always been a complicated and evolving combination of Western mores and classic polygamous patterns. Like Western companionate marriage, Mormon polygamy condemns extramarital sex. Yet historically, like its non-Western counterparts, it deemphasized romantic love. Even so, jealousy was always a problem. One study puts the rate of 19th-century polygamous divorce at triple the rate for monogamous families. Unlike their forebears, contemporary Mormon polygamists try to combine polygamy with companionate marriage—and have a very tough time of it. We have no definitive figures, but divorce is frequent. Irwin Altman and Joseph Ginat, who've written the most detailed account of today's breakaway Mormon polygamist sects, highlight the special stresses put on families trying to combine modern notions of romantic love with polygamy. Strict religious rules of parity among wives make the effort to create a hybrid traditionalist/modern version of Mormon polygamy at least plausible, if very stressful. But polygamy let loose in modern secular America would destroy our understanding of marital fidelity, while putting nothing viable in its place. And postmodern polygamy is a lot closer than you think.

Polyamory

America's new, souped-up version of polygamy is called "polyamory." Polyamorists trace their descent from the anti-monogamy movements of the sixties and seventies—everything from hippie communes, to the support groups that grew up around Robert Rimmer's 1966 novel "The Harrad Experiment," to the cult of Bhagwan Shree Rajneesh. Polyamorists proselytize for "responsible non-monogamy"—open, loving, and stable sexual relationships among more than two people. The modern polyamory movement took off in the mid-nineties—partly because of the growth of the Internet (with its confidentiality), but also in parallel to, and inspired by, the rising gay marriage movement.

Unlike classic polygamy, which features one man and several women, polyamory comprises a bewildering variety of sexual combinations. There are triads of one woman and two men; heterosexual group marriages; groups in which some or all members are bisexual; lesbian groups, and so forth. (For details, see Deborah Anapol's "Polyamory: The New Love Without Limits," one of the movement's authoritative guides, or Google the word polyamory.)

Once monogamy is defined out of marriage, it will be next to impossible to educate a new generation in what it takes to keep companionate marriage intact.

Supposedly, polyamory is not a synonym for promiscuity. In practice, though, there is a continuum between polyamory and "swinging." Swinging couples dally with multiple sexual partners while intentionally avoiding emotional entanglements. Polyamorists, in contrast, try to establish stable emotional ties among a sexually connected group. Although the subcultures of swinging and polyamory are recognizably different, many individuals move freely between them. And since polyamorous group marriages can be sexually closed or open, it's often tough to draw a line between polyamory and swinging. Here, then, is the modern American version of Nigeria's extramarital polygamous promiscuity. Once the principles of monogamous companionate marriage are breached, even for supposedly stable and committed sexual groups, the slide toward full-fledged promiscuity is difficult to halt.

Polyamorists are enthusiastic proponents of same-sex marriage. Obviously, any attempt to restrict marriage to a single man and woman would prevent the legalization of polyamory. After passage of the Defense of Marriage Act in 1996, an article appeared in *Loving More*, the flagship magazine of the polyamory movement, calling for the creation of a polyamorist rights movement modeled on the movement for gay rights. The piece was published under the pen name Joy Singer, identified as the graduate of a "top ten law school" and a political organizer and public official in California for the previous two decades.

Taking a leaf from the gay marriage movement, Singer suggested starting small. A campaign for hospital visitation rights for polyamorous spouses would be the way to begin. Full marriage and adoption rights would come later. Again using the gay marriage movement as a model, Singer called for careful selection of acceptable public spokesmen (i.e., people from longstanding poly families with children). Singer even published a speech by Iowa state legislator Ed Fallon on behalf of gay marriage, arguing that the goal would be to get a congressman to give exactly the same speech as Fallon, but substituting the word "poly" for "gay" throughout. Try telling polyamorists that the link between gay marriage and group marriage is a mirage.

The flexible, egalitarian, and altogether postmodern polyamorists are more likely to influence the larger society than Mormon polygamists. The polyamorists go after monogamy in a way that resonates with America's secular, post-sixties culture. Yet the fundamental drawback is the same for Mormons and polyamorists alike. Polyamory websites are filled with chatter about jealousy, the problem that will not go away. Inevitably, group marriages based on modern principles of companionate love, without religious roles and restraints, are unstable. Like the short-lived hippie communes, group marriages will be broken on the contradiction between companionate love and group solidarity. And children will pay the price. The harms of state-sanctioned polyamorous marriage would extend well beyond the polyamorists themselves. Once monogamy is defined out of marriage, it will be next to impossible to educate a new generation in what it takes to keep companionate marriage intact. State-sanctioned polyamory would spell the effective end of marriage. And that is precisely what polyamory's new—and surprisingly influential—defenders are aiming for.

The family law radicals

State-sanctioned polyamory is now the cutting-edge issue among scholars of family law. The preeminent school of thought in academic family law has its origins in the arguments of radical gay activists who once *opposed* same-sex marriage. In the early nineties, radicals like longtime National Gay and Lesbian Task Force policy director Paula Ettelbrick spoke out against making legal marriage a priority for the gay rights movement. Marriage, Ettelbrick reminded her fellow activists, "has long been the focus of radical feminist revulsion." Encouraging gays to marry, said Ettelbrick, would only force gay "assimilation" to American norms, when the real object of the gay rights movement ought to be getting Americans to accept gay difference. "Being queer," said Ettelbrick, "means pushing the parameters of sex and family, and in the process transforming the very fabric of society."

Promoting polyamory is the ideal way to "radically reorder society's view of the family," and Ettelbrick, who has since formally signed on as a supporter of gay marriage (and is frequently quoted by the press), is now part of a movement that hopes to use gay marriage as an opening to press for state-sanctioned polyamory. Ettelbrick teaches law at the University of Michigan, New York University, Barnard, and Columbia. She has a lot of company.

> *The increased openness of homosexual partnerships is slowly collapsing the taboo against polygamy and polyamory.*

Nancy Polikoff is a professor at American University's law school. In 1993, Polikoff published a powerful and radical critique of gay marriage. Polikoff stressed that during the height of the lesbian feminist movement of the seventies, even many heterosexual feminists refused to marry because they believed marriage to be an inherently patriarchal and oppressive institution. A movement for gay marriage, warned Polikoff, would surely promote marriage as a social good, trotting out monogamous couples as spokesmen in a way that would marginalize non-monogamous gays and would fail to challenge the legitimacy of marriage itself. Like Ettelbrick, Polikoff now supports the right of gays to marry. And like Ettelbrick, Polikoff is part of a movement whose larger goal is to use legal gay marriage to push for state-sanctioned polyamory—the ultimate subversion of marriage itself. Polikoff and Ettelbrick represent what is arguably now the dominant perspective within the discipline of family law.

Not only could heterosexual couples register as official partners, so could gay couples, adult children living with parents, and siblings or friends sharing a house.

Cornell University law professor Martha Fineman is another key figure in the field of family law. In her 1995 book "The Neutered Mother, the Sexual Family, and Other Twentieth Century Tragedies," she argued for the abolition of marriage as a legal category. Fineman's book begins with her recollection of an experience from the late seventies in politically radical Madison, Wisconsin. To her frustration, she could not convince even the most progressive members of Madison's Equal Opportunities Commission to recognize "plural sexual groupings" as marriages. That failure helped energize Fineman's lifelong drive to abolish marriage.

State-sanctioned polyamory

But it's University of Utah law professor Martha Ertman who stands on the cutting edge of family law. Building on Fineman's proposals for the abolition of legal marriage, Ertman has offered a legal template for a sweeping relationship contract system modeled on corporate law. Ertman wants state-sanctioned polyamory, legally organized on the model of limited liability companies.

In arguing for the replacement of marriage with a contract system that accommodates polyamory, Ertman notes that legal and social hostility to polygamy and polyamory are decreasing. She goes on astutely to imply that the increased openness of homosexual partnerships is slowly collapsing the taboo against polygamy and polyamory. And Ertman is frank about the purpose of her proposed reform—to render the distinction between traditional marriage and polyamory "morally neutral."

A sociologist rather than a professor of law, Judith Stacey, the Barbra Streisand Professor in Contemporary Gender Studies at USC, is another key member of this group. Stacey has long championed alternative family forms. Her current research is on gay families consisting of more than two adults, whose several members consider themselves either married or contractually bound.

In 1996, in the *Michigan Law Review*, David Chambers, a professor of law at the University of Michigan and another prominent member of this group, explained why radical opponents of marriage ought to support gay marriage. Rather than reinforcing a two-person definition of marriage, argued Chambers, gay marriage would make society more accepting of further legal changes. "By ceasing to conceive of marriage as a partnership composed of one person of each sex, the state may become more receptive to units of three or more."

Gradual transition from gay marriage to state-sanctioned polyamory, and the eventual abolition of marriage itself as a legal category, is now the most influential paradigm within academic family law. As Chambers put it, "All desirable changes in family law need not be made at once."

Redefining families

Finally, Martha Minow of Harvard Law School deserves mention. Minow has not advocated state-sanctioned polygamy or polyamory, but the principles she champions pave the way for both. Minow argues that families need to be radically redefined, putting blood ties and traditional legal arrangements aside and attending instead to the functional realities of new family configurations.

Ettelbrick, Polikoff, Fineman, Ertman, Stacey, Chambers, and Minow are among the most prominent family law theorists in the country. They have plenty of followers and hold much of the power and initiative within their field. There may be other approaches to academic family law, but none exceed the radicals in influence. In the last couple of years, there have been a number of conferences on family law dominated by the views of this school. The conferences have names like "Marriage Law: Obsolete or Cutting Edge?" and "Assimilation & Resistance: Emerging Issues in Law & Sexuality." The titles turn on the paradox of using marriage, seemingly a conservative path toward assimilation, as a tool of radical cultural "resistance."

One of the most important recent family law meetings was the March 2003 Hofstra conference on "Marriage, Democracy, and Families." The radicals were out in full force. On a panel entitled "Intimate Affiliation and Democracy: Beyond Marriage?" Fineman, Ertman, and Stacey held forth on polyamory, the legal abolition of marriage, and related issues. Although there were more moderate scholars present, there was barely a challenge to the radicals' suggestion that it was time to move "beyond marriage." The few traditionalists in family law are relatively isolated. Many, maybe most, of the prominent figures in family law count themselves as advocates for lesbian and gay rights. Yet family law today is as influenced by the hostility to marriage of seventies feminism as it is by advocacy for gay rights. It is this confluence of radical feminism and gay rights that now shapes the field.

Beyond conjugality

You might think the radicals who dominate the discipline of family law are just a bunch of eccentric and irrelevant academics. You would be wrong. For one thing, there is already a thriving non-profit organization, the Alternatives to Marriage Project, that advances the radicals' goals. When controversies over the family hit the news, experts provided by the Alternatives to Marriage Project are often quoted in mainstream media outlets. While the Alternatives to Marriage Project endorses gay marriage, its longer-term goal is to replace marriage with a system that recognizes "the full range" of family types.

That includes polyamorous families. The Alternatives to Marriage Project's statement of purpose—its "Affirmation of Family Diversity"—is signed not only by Ettelbrick, Polikoff, and Stacey but by several polyamorists as well. On a list of signatories that includes academic luminaries like Yale historian Nancy Cott, you can find Barry Northrup of *Loving More* magazine. The Alternatives to Marriage Project, along with Martha Ertman's pioneering legal proposals, has given polyamory a foothold on respectability.

The first real public triumph of the family law radicals has come in Canada. In 1997, the Canadian Parliament established the Law Commission of Canada to serve Parliament and the Justice Ministry as a kind of advisory board on legal reform. In December 2001, the commission submitted a report to Parliament called "Beyond Conjugality," which stops just short of recommending the abolition of marriage in Canada.

"Beyond Conjugality" contains three basic recommendations. First, judges are directed to concentrate on whether the individuals before them are "functionally interdependent," regardless of their actual marital status. On that theory, a household consisting of an adult child still living with his mother might be treated as the functional equivalent of a married couple. In so disregarding marital status, "Beyond Conjugality" is clearly drawing on the work of Minow, whose writings are listed in the bibliography.

"Beyond Conjugality"'s second key recommendation is that a legal structure be established allowing people to register their personal relationships with the government. Not only could heterosexual couples register as official partners, so could gay couples, adult children living with parents, and siblings or friends sharing a house. Although the authors of "Beyond Conjugality" are politic enough to relegate the point to footnotes, they state that they see no reason, in principle, to limit registered partnerships to two people.

The final recommendation of "Beyond Conjugality"—legalization of same-sex marriage—drew the most publicity when the report was released. Yet for the Law Commission of Canada, same-sex marriage is clearly just one part of the larger project of doing away with marriage itself. "Beyond Conjugality" stops short of recommending the abolition of legal marriage. The authors glumly note that, for the moment, the public is unlikely to accept such a step.

The powerful radical influence

The text of "Beyond Conjugality," its bibliography, and the Law Commission of Canada's other publications unmistakably reveal the influence of the radical theorists who now dominate the discipline of family law. While Canada's parliament has postponed action on "Beyond Conjugality," the report has already begun to shape the culture. The decision by the Canadian government in June 2003 not to contest court rulings legalizing gay marriage is only the beginning of the changes that Canada's judges and legal bureaucrats have in mind. The simultaneity of the many reforms is striking. Gay marriage is being pressed, but in tandem with a registration system that will sanction polyamorous unions, and eventually replace marriage itself. Empirically, the radicals' hopes are being validated. Gay marriage is not strengthening marriage but has instead become part of a larger unraveling of traditional marriage laws.

Ah, but that's Canada, you say. Yet America has its rough equivalent of the Law Commission of Canada—the American Law Institute (ALI), an organization of legal scholars whose recommendations commonly shape important legal reforms. In 2000, ALI promulgated a report called "Principles of the Law of Family Dissolution" recommending that judges effectively disregard the distinction between married couples and longtime cohabitors. While the ALI principles do not go so far as to set up a system of partnership registration to replace marriage, the report's framework for recognizing a wide variety of cohabiting partnerships puts it on the same path as "Beyond Conjugality."

What if, instead of marriage reducing gay promiscuity, sexually open gay couples help redefine marriage as a non-monogamous institution?

Collapsing the distinction between cohabitation and marriage is a proposal especially damaging to children, who are decidedly better off when born to married parents. (This aspect of the ALI report has been persuasively criticized by Kay Hymowitz, in the March 2003 issue of *Commentary*.) But a more disturbing aspect of the ALI report is its evasion of the polygamy and polyamory issues.

Prior to publication of the ALI Principles, the report's authors were pressed (at the 2000 annual meeting of the American Law Institute) about the question of polygamy. The authors put off the controversy by defining legal cohabitors as couples. Yet the ALI report offers no principled way of excluding polyamorous or polygamous cohabitors from recognition. The report's reforms are said to be based on the need to recognize "statistically growing" patterns of relationship. By this standard, the growth of polyamorous cohabitation will soon require the legal recognition of polyamory.

Although America's ALI Principles do not follow Canada's "Beyond Conjugality" in proposing either state-sanctioned polyamory or the outright end of marriage, the University of Utah's Martha Ertman has suggested that the American Law Institute is intentionally holding back on more radical proposals for pragmatic political reasons. Certainly, the ALI Principles' authors take Canadian law as the model for the report's most radical provisions.

Further confirmation, if any were needed, of the mainstream influence of the family law radicals came with Al and Tipper Gore's 2002 book *Joined at the Heart*, in which they define a family as those who are "joined at the heart" (rather than by blood or by law). The notion that a family is any group "joined at the heart" comes straight from Harvard's Martha Minow, who worked with the Gores. In fact, the Minow article from which the Gores take their definition of family is also the article in which Minow tentatively floats the idea of substituting domestic partnership registries for traditional marriage. So one of the guiding spirits of Canada's "Beyond Conjugality" report almost had a friend in the White House.

Gay men and monogamy

Polygamy, polyamory, and the abolition of marriage are bad ideas. But what has that got to do with gay marriage? The reason these ideas are connected is that gay marriage is increasingly being treated as a civil rights issue. Once we say that gay couples have a right to have their commitments recognized by the state, it becomes next to impossible to deny that same right to polygamists, polyamorists, or even cohabiting relatives and friends. And once everyone's relationship is recognized, marriage is gone, and only a system of flexible relationship contracts is left. The only way to stop gay marriage from launching a slide down this slope is if there is a compelling state interest in blocking polygamy or polyamory that does not also apply to gay marriage. Many would agree that the state has a compelling interest in preventing polygamy and polyamory from undermining the ethos of monogamy at the core of marriage. The trouble is, gay marriage itself threatens the ethos of monogamy.

The "conservative" case for gay marriage holds that state-sanctioned marriage will reduce gay male promiscuity. But what if the effect works in reverse? What if, instead of marriage reducing gay promiscuity, sexually open gay couples help redefine marriage as a non-monogamous institution? There is evidence that this is exactly what will happen.

> *While gay men in civil unions were more likely to affirm monogamy than gays outside of civil unions, gay men in civil unions were far less supportive of monogamy than heterosexual married men.*

Consider sociologist Gretchen Stiers's 1998 study "From This Day Forward" (Stiers favors gay marriage, and calls herself a lesbian "queer theorist"). "From This Day Forward" reports that while exceedingly few of even the most committed gay and lesbian couples surveyed believe that marriage will strengthen and stabilize their personal relationships, nearly half of the surveyed couples who actually disdain traditional marriage (and even gay commitment ceremonies) will nonetheless get married. Why? For the financial and legal benefits of marriage. And Stiers's study suggests that many radical gays and lesbians who yearn to see marriage abolished (and multiple sexual unions legitimized) intend to marry, not only as a way of securing benefits but as part of a self-conscious attempt to subvert the institution of marriage. Stiers's study suggests that the "subversive" intentions of the radical legal theorists are shared by a significant portion of the gay community itself.

Stiers's study was focused on the most committed gay couples. Yet even in a sample with a disproportionate number of male couples who had gone through a commitment ceremony (and Stiers had to go out of her research protocol just to find enough male couples to balance the committed lesbian couples) nearly 20 percent of the men questioned did not practice monogamy. In a representative sample of gay male couples, that number would be vastly higher. More significantly, a mere 10 percent of even this skewed sample of gay men mentioned monogamy as an important aspect of commitment (meaning that even many of those men who had undergone "union ceremonies" failed to identify fidelity with commitment). And these, the very most committed gay male couples, are the ones who will be trailblazing marital norms for their peers, and exemplifying gay marriage for the nation. So concerns about the effects of gay marriage on the social ideal of marital monogamy seem justified.

A recent survey of gay couples in civil unions by University of Vermont psychologists Esther Rothblum and Sondra Solomon confirms what Stiers's study suggests—that married gay male couples will be far less likely than married heterosexual couples to identify marriage with monogamy. Rothblum and Solomon contacted all 2,300 couples who entered civil unions in Vermont between June 1, 2000, and June 30, 2001. More than 300 civil union couples residing in and out of the state responded. Rothblum and Solomon then compared the gay couples in civil unions with heterosexual couples and gay couples outside of civil unions. Among married heterosexual men, 79 percent felt that marriage demanded monogamy, 50 percent of men in gay civil unions insisted on monogamy, while only 34 percent of gay men outside of civil unions affirmed monogamy.

> *Once lesbian couples can marry, there will be a powerful legal case for extending parental recognition to triumvirates.*

While gay men in civil unions were more likely to affirm monogamy than gays outside of civil unions, gay men in civil unions were far less supportive of monogamy than heterosexual married men. That discrepancy may well be significantly greater under gay marriage than under civil unions. That's because of the effect identified by Stiers—the likelihood that many gays who do not value the traditional monogamous ethos of marriage will marry anyway for the financial benefits that marriage can bring. (A full 86 percent of the civil unions couples who responded to the Rothblum-Solomon survey live outside Vermont, and therefore receive no financial benefits from their new legal status.) The Rothblum-Solomon study may also undercount heterosexual married male acceptance of monogamy, since one member of all the married heterosexual couples in the survey was the sibling of a gay man in a civil union, and thus more likely to be socially liberal than most heterosexuals.

Even moderate gay advocates of same-sex marriage grant that, at present, gay male relationships are far less monogamous than heterosexual relationships. And there is a persuasive literature on this subject: Gabriel Rotello's "Sexual Ecology," for example, offers a documented and powerful account of the behavioral and ideological barriers to monogamy among gay men. The moderate advocates say marriage will change this reality. But they ignore, or downplay, the possibility that gay marriage will change marriage more than it changes the men who marry. Married gay couples will begin to redefine the meaning of marriage for the culture as a whole, in part by removing monogamy as an essential component of marriage. No doubt, the process will be pushed along by cutting-edge movies and TV shows that tout the new "open" marriages being pioneered by gay spouses. In fact, author and gay marriage advocate Richard Mohr has long expressed the hope and expectation that legal gay marriage will succeed in defining monogamy out of marriage.

Lesbians and triple parenting

Lesbians, for their part, do value monogamy. Over 82 percent of the women in the Rothblum-Solomon study, for example, insisted on monogamy, regardless of sexual orientation or marital status. Yet lesbian marriage will undermine the connection between marriage and monogamy in a different way. Lesbians who bear children with sperm donors sometimes set up de facto three-parent families. Typically, these families include a sexually bound lesbian couple, and a male biological father who is close to the couple but not sexually involved. Once lesbian couples can marry, there will be a powerful legal case for extending parental recognition to triumvirates. It will be difficult to question the parental credentials of a sperm donor, or of a married, lesbian non–birth mother spouse who helps to raise a child from birth. And just as the argument for gay marriage has been built upon the right to gay adoption, legally recognized triple parenting will eventually usher in state-sanctioned triple (and therefore group) marriage.

This year, there was a triple parenting case in Canada involving a lesbian couple and a sperm donor. The judge made it clear that he wanted to assign parental status to all three adults but held back because he said he lacked jurisdiction. On this issue, the United States is already in "advance" of Canada. Martha Ertman is now pointing to a 2000 Minnesota case (*La Chapelle v. Mitten*) in which a court did grant parental rights to lesbian partners and a sperm donor. Ertman argues that this case creates a legal precedent for state-sanctioned polyamory.

Gay marriages of convenience

Ironically, the form of gay matrimony that may pose the greatest threat to the institution of marriage involves heterosexuals. A Brigham Young University professor, Alan J. Hawkins, suggests an all-too-likely scenario in which two heterosexuals of the same sex might marry as a way of obtaining financial benefits. Consider the plight of an underemployed and uninsured single mother in her early 30s who sees little real prospect of marriage (to a man) in her future. Suppose she has a good friend, also female and heterosexual, who is single and childless but employed with good spousal benefits. Sooner or later, friends like this are going to start contracting same-sex marriages of convenience. The single mom will get medical and governmental benefits, will share her friend's paycheck, and will gain an additional caretaker for the kids besides. Her friend will gain companionship and a family life. The marriage would obviously be sexually open. And if lightning struck and the right man came along for one of the women, they could always divorce and marry heterosexually.

In a narrow sense, the women and children in this arrangement would be better off. Yet the larger effects of such unions on the institution of marriage would be devastating. At a stroke, marriage would be severed not only from the complementarity of the sexes but also from its connection to romance and sexual exclusivity—and even from the hope of permanence. In Hawkins's words, the proliferation of such arrangements "would turn marriage into the moral equivalent of a Social Security benefit." The effect would be to further diminish the sense that a woman ought to be married to the father of her children. In the aggregate, what we now call out-of-wedlock births would increase. And the connection between marriage and sexual fidelity would be nonexistent.

> *Marriage will have been severed from monogamy, from sexuality, and even from the dream of permanence.*

Hawkins thinks gay marriages of convenience would be contracted in significant numbers—certainly enough to draw the attention of a media eager to tout such unions as the hip, postmodern marriages of the moment. Hawkins also believes that these unions of convenience could begin to undermine marriage's institutional foundations fairly quickly. He may be right. The gay marriage movement took more than a decade to catch fire. A movement for state-sanctioned polygamy-polyamory could take as long. And the effects of sexually open gay marriages on the ethos of monogamy will similarly occur over time. But any degree of publicity for same-sex marriages of convenience could have dramatic effects. Without further legal ado, same-sex marriages of convenience will realize the radicals' fondest hopes. Marriage will have been severed from monogamy, from sexuality, and even from the dream of permanence. Which would bring us virtually to the bottom of the slippery slope.

We are far closer to that day than anyone realizes. Does the Supreme Court's defense of sexual liberty . . . in the *Lawrence v. Texas* sodomy case mean that, short of a constitutional amendment, gay marriage is inevitable? Perhaps not. Justice Scalia was surely correct to warn in his dissent that Lawrence greatly weakens the legal barriers to gay marriage. Sodomy laws, although rarely enforced, did provide a public policy basis on which a state could refuse to recognize a gay marriage performed in another state. Now the grounds for that "public policy exception" have been eroded. And as Scalia warned, *Lawrence*'s sweeping guarantees of personal autonomy in matters of sex could easily be extended to the question of who a person might choose to marry.

So it is true that, given *Lawrence*, the legal barriers to gay marriage are now hanging by a thread. Nonetheless, in an important respect, Scalia underestimated the resources for a successful legal argument against gay marriage. True, *Lawrence* eliminates moral disapprobation as an acceptable, rational basis for public policy distinctions between homosexuality and heterosexuality. But that doesn't mean there is no rational basis for blocking either same-sex marriage or polygamy.

Children need traditional families

There is a rational basis for blocking both gay marriage and polygamy, and it does not depend upon a vague or religiously based disapproval of homosexuality or polygamy. Children need the stable family environment provided by marriage. In our individualist Western society, marriage must be companionate—and therefore monogamous. Monogamy will be undermined by gay marriage itself, and by gay marriage's ushering in of polygamy and polyamory.

This argument ought to be sufficient to pass the test of rational scrutiny set by the Supreme Court in *Lawrence v. Texas*. Certainly, the slippery slope argument was at the center of the legislative debate on the federal Defense of Marriage Act, and so should protect that act from being voided on the same grounds as Texas's sodomy law. But of course, given the majority's sweeping declarations in *Lawrence*, and the hostility of the legal elite to traditional marriage, it may well be foolish to rely on the Supreme Court to uphold either state or federal Defense of Marriage Acts.

This is the case, in a nutshell, for something like the proposed Federal Marriage Amendment to the Constitution, which would define marriage as the union of a man and a woman. At a stroke, such an amendment would block gay marriage, polygamy, polyamory, and the replacement of marriage by a contract system. Whatever the courts might make of the slippery slope argument, the broader public will take it seriously. Since *Lawrence*, we have already heard from Jon Carroll in the *San Francisco Chronicle* calling for legalized polygamy. Judith Levine in the *Village Voice* has made a plea for group marriage. And Michael Kinsley—no queer theorist but a completely mainstream journalist—has publicly called for the legal abolition of marriage. So the most radical proposal of all has now moved out of the law schools and legal commissions, and onto the front burner of public discussion.

Fair-minded people differ on the matter of homosexuality. I happen to think that sodomy laws should have been repealed (although legislatively). I also believe that our increased social tolerance for homosexuality is generally a good thing. But the core issue here is not homosexuality; it is marriage. Marriage is a critical social institution. Stable families depend on it. Society depends on stable families. Up to now, with all the changes in marriage, the one thing we've been sure of is that marriage means monogamy. Gay marriage will break that connection. It will do this by itself, and by leading to polygamy and polyamory. What lies beyond gay marriage is no marriage at all.

2

Homophobia
Threatens Families

Sharon Underwood

The mother of a gay son, Sharon Underwood wrote this letter to the Valley News, *a newspaper published in West Lebanon, New Hampshire.*

The very people who claim that homosexuality threatens families are the ones who harm families through their hateful rhetoric. The misguided, righteous arguments about the supposed "homosexual menace" are born out of ignorance and cruelty. Myths perpetuated by religious hypocrites need to be corrected. Accepting homosexuality is not equivalent to promoting pedophilia, and being gay is not a choice—it is inborn. Moreover, God does not condemn gay people and gay people are not "outsiders" who are invading our communities—they are an integral part of our society. It is time that we granted our gay citizens the same rights and opportunities for happiness that heterosexual citizens enjoy.

M any letters have been sent to the Forum concerning the homosexual menace in our state. I am the mother of a gay son and I've taken enough from you good people.

I'm tired of your foolish rhetoric about the "homosexual agenda" and your allegations that accepting homosexuality is the same thing as advocating sex with children. You are cruel and you are ignorant. You have been robbing me of the joys of motherhood ever since my children were tiny. My firstborn son started suffering at the hands of the moral little thugs from your moral, upright families from the time he was in the first grade. He was physically and verbally abused from first grade straight through high school because he was perceived to be gay. He never professed to be gay or had any association with anything gay, but he had the misfortune not to walk or have gestures like the other boys. He was called "fag" incessantly, starting when he was six.

In high school, while your children were doing what kids that age should be doing, mine labored over a suicide note, drafting and redrafting it to be sure his family knew how much he loved them. My sobbing

17-year-old tore the heart out of me as he choked out that he just couldn't bear to continue living any longer, that he didn't want to be gay and that he couldn't face a life with no dignity.

You have the audacity to talk about protecting families and children from the homosexual menace, while you yourselves tear apart families and drive children to despair. I don't know why my son is gay, but I do know that God didn't put him, and millions like him, on this Earth to give you someone to abuse. God gave you brains so that you could think, and it's about time you started doing that.

At the core of all your misguided beliefs is the belief that this could never happen to you, that there is some kind of subculture out there that people have chosen to join. The fact is that if it can happen to my family, it can happen to yours, and you won't get to choose. Whether it is genetic or whether something occurs during a critical time of fetal development, I don't know. I can only tell you with an absolute certainty that it is inborn.

You have the audacity to talk about protecting families and children from the homosexual menace, while you yourselves tear apart families and drive children to despair.

If you want to tout your own morality, you'd best come up with something more substantive than your heterosexuality. You did nothing to earn it; it was given to you. If you disagree, I would be interested in hearing your story, because my own heterosexuality was a blessing I received with no effort whatsoever on my part. It is so woven into the very soul of me that nothing could ever change it. For those of you who reduce sexual orientation to a simple choice, a character issue, a bad habit or something that can be changed by a 10-step program, I'm puzzled. Are you saying that your own sexual orientation is nothing more than something you have chosen, that you could change it at will? If that's not the case, then why would you suggest that someone else could?

Gays and lesbians are part of our community

A popular theme in your letters is that Vermont has been infiltrated by outsiders. Both sides of my family have lived in Vermont for generations. I am heart and soul a Vermonter, so I'll thank you to stop saying that you are speaking for "true Vermonters." You invoke the memory of the brave people who have fought on the battlefield for this great country, saying that they didn't give their lives so that the "homosexual agenda" could tear down the principles they died defending. My 83-year-old father fought in some of the most horrific battles of World War II, was wounded and awarded the Purple Heart. He shakes his head in sadness at the life his grandson has had to live. He says he fought alongside homosexuals in those battles, that they did their part and bothered no one. One of his best friends in the service was gay, and he never knew it until the end, and when he did find out, it mattered not at all. That wasn't the measure of the man. You religious folk just can't bear the thought that as my son emerges from the hell that was his childhood he might like to find a life-long companion and have a measure of happiness. It offends your sensibilities that he should request the right to visit that companion in the hospital, to make medical decisions for him or to benefit from tax laws governing inheritance. How dare he . . . these outrageous requests would threaten the very existence of your family, would undermine the sanctity of marriage.

You use religion to abdicate your responsibility to be thinking human beings. There are vast numbers of religious people who find your attitudes repugnant. God is not for the privileged majority, and God knows my son has committed no sin.

The deep-thinking author of a letter to the Forum on April 12 who lectures about homosexual sin and tells us about "those of us who have been blessed with the benefits of a religious upbringing" asks: "What ever happened to the idea of striving . . . to be better human beings than we are?"

Indeed, sir, what ever happened to that?

3

Gay Parenting Places Children at Risk

Tim Dailey

Tim Dailey is a senior fellow in culture studies at the Family Research Council, a conservative organization that promotes public policy based on Judeo-Christian values and traditional definitions of marriage and the family.

Research claiming that children thrive in gay and lesbian households can only be described as flawed and misleading. The studies supporting homosexual parenting are full of methodological and design errors that lead to unfounded conclusions. In truth, same-sex households expose children to harmful aspects of the homosexual lifestyle, including promiscuity, health hazards, family violence, incest, substance abuse, and sexual identity confusion. Gay and lesbian activists want to undermine the very definition of marriage by attacking monogamy, commitment, and chastity. Children fare much better in traditional families where they receive appropriate discipline, attention, and moral and spiritual guidance.

A number of studies in recent years have purported to show that children raised in gay and lesbian households fare no worse than those reared in traditional families. Yet much of that research fails to meet acceptable standards for psychological research; it is compromised by methodological flaws and driven by political agendas instead of an objective search for truth. In addition, openly lesbian researchers sometimes conduct research with an interest in portraying homosexual parenting in a positive light. The deficiencies of studies on homosexual parenting include reliance upon an inadequate sample size, lack of random sampling, lack of anonymity of research participants, and self-presentation bias.

The presence of methodological defects—a mark of substandard research—would be cause for rejection of research conducted in virtually any other subject area. The overlooking of such deficiencies in research papers on homosexual failures can be attributed to the "politically correct" determination within those in the social science professions to "prove"

Tim Dailey, "Homosexual Parenting: Placing Children at Risk," Family Research Council, *Insight*, October 30, 2001. Copyright © 2001 by the Family Research Council. All rights reserved. Reproduced by permission. www.frc.org. 1-800-225-4008, 801 G St. NW, Washington, DC 20001.

that homosexual households are no different than traditional families.

However, no amount of scholarly legerdemain contained in an accumulation of flawed studies can obscure the well-established and growing body of evidence showing that both mothers and fathers provide unique and irreplaceable contributions to the raising of children. Children raised in traditional families by a mother and father are happier, healthier, and more successful than children raised in non-traditional environments.

A faulty foundation of research

David Cramer, whose review of twenty studies on homosexual parenting appeared in the *Journal of Counseling and Development*, found the following:

> The generalizability of the studies is limited. Few studies employed control groups and most had small samples. Almost all parents were Anglo-American, middle class, and well educated. Measures for assessing gender roles in young children tend to focus on social behavior and generally are not accurate psychological instruments. Therefore it is impossible to make large scale generalizations . . . that would be applicable to all children.

Since these words were penned in 1986, the number of studies on the subject of homosexual parenting has steadily grown. The fact that these studies continue to be flawed by the methodological errors warned about by Cramer has not inhibited the proponents of homosexual parenting from their sanguine assessment of the outcomes of children raised in homosexual households.

Louise B. Silverstein and Carl F. Auerbach, for example, see no essential difference between traditional mother-father families and homosexual-led families: "Other aspects of personal development and social relationships were also found to be within the normal range for children raised in lesbian and gay families." They suggest that "gay and lesbian parents can create a positive family context."

This conclusion is echoed in the official statement on homosexual parenting by the American Psychological Association's Public Interest Directorate, authored by openly lesbian activist Charlotte J. Patterson of the University of Virginia:

> In summary, there is no evidence that lesbians and gay men are unfit to be parents or that psychosocial development among children of gay men or lesbians is compromised in any respect. . . . Not a single study has found children of gay or lesbian parents to be disadvantaged in any significant respect relative to children of heterosexual parents.

Problems with homosexual parenting research

Upon closer examination, however, this conclusion is not as confident as it appears. In the next paragraph, Patterson qualifies her statement. Echoing Cramer's concern from a decade earlier, she writes: "It should be acknowledged that research on lesbian and gay parents and their children is still very new and relatively scarce. . . . Longitudinal studies that follow lesbian and gay families over time are badly needed." The years have passed since Patterson's admission of the inadequacy of homosexual parenting studies, and we still await definitive, objective research substantiating her claims.

In addition, Patterson acknowledges that "research in this area has presented a variety of methodological challenges," and that "questions have been raised with regard to sampling issues, statistical power, and other technical matters." She adds, revealingly:

> Research in this area has also been criticized for using poorly matched or no control groups in designs that call for such controls. . . . Other criticisms have been that most studies have involved relatively small samples [and] that there have been inadequacies in assessment procedures employed in some studies.

Though she admits to serious methodological and design errors that would call into question the findings of any study, Patterson makes the astonishing claim that "even with all the questions and/or limitations that may characterize research in the area, none of the published research suggests conclusions different from those that will be summarized below." But any such conclusions are only as reliable as the evidence upon which they are based. If the alleged evidence is flawed, then the conclusions must likewise be considered suspect.

"The conclusion that there are no significant differences in children raised by lesbian mothers versus heterosexual mothers is not supported by the published research data base."

One suspects that the lack of studies with proper design and controls is due to the political agendas driving the acceptance of homosexual parenting, which favor inadequate and superficial research yielding the desired results.

In a study published in the *Journal of Divorce and Remarriage*, P.A. Belcastro et al. reviewed fourteen studies on homosexual parenting according to accepted scientific standards. Their "most impressive finding" was that "all of the studies lacked external validity. The conclusion that there are no significant differences in children raised by lesbian mothers versus heterosexual mothers is not supported by the published research data base." Similarly, in their study of lesbian couples in *Family Relations*, L. Keopke et al. remark, "Conducting research in the gay community is fraught with methodological problems."

A careful reading of studies used to lend support to homosexual parenting reveals more modest claims than are often attributed to them, as well as significant methodological limitations:

> Nearly all of the existing studies of homosexual parenting have major deficiencies in sampling: They use a small sam-

ple size; they fail to obtain a truly representative sample due to sources of sampling bias; they do not use a random sample; or they use a sample with characteristics that are inappropriate for the crucial development research question involved in the study. . . .

Harmful aspects of the homosexual lifestyle

The evidence demonstrates incontrovertibly that the homosexual lifestyle is inconsistent with the proper raising of children. Homosexual relationships are characteristically unstable and are fundamentally incapable of providing children the security they need.

Homosexual Promiscuity.

Studies indicate that the average male homosexual has hundreds of sex partners in his lifetime, a lifestyle that is difficult for even "committed" homosexuals to break free of and which is not conducive to a healthy and wholesome atmosphere for the raising of children.

• A.P. Bell and M.S. Weinberg, in their classic study of male and female homosexuality, found that 43 percent of white male homosexuals had sex with five hundred or more partners, with 28 percent having 1,000 or more sex partners.

• In their study of the sexual profiles of 2,583 older homosexuals published in *Journal of Sex Research*, Paul Van de Ven et al. found that "the modal range for number of sexual partners ever [of homosexuals] was 101–500." In addition, 10.2 percent to 15.7 percent had between 501 and 1000 partners. A further 10.2 percent to 15.7 percent reported having had more than 1000 lifetime sexual partners.

• A survey conducted by the homosexual magazine *Genre* found that 24 percent of the respondents said they had had more than 100 sexual partners in their lifetime. The magazine noted that several respondents suggested including a category of those who had more than 1,000 sexual partners.

• In his study of male homosexuality in *Western Sexuality: Practice and Precept in Past and Present Times*, M. Pollak found that "few homosexual relationships last longer than two years, with many men reporting hundreds of lifetime partners."

The meaning of "committed" typically means something radically different than in heterosexual marriage.

Promiscuity Among Homosexual Couples.

Even in those homosexual relationships in which the partners consider themselves to be in a committed relationship, the meaning of "committed" typically means something radically different than in heterosexual marriage.

• In *The Male Couple*, authors David P. McWhirter and Andrew M. Mattison report that in a study of 156 males in homosexual relationships lasting from one to thirty-seven years:

Only seven couples have a totally exclusive sexual relationship, and these men all have been together for less than five
years. Stated another way, all couples with a relationship
lasting more than five years have incorporated some provision for outside sexual activity in their relationships.

Most understood sexual relations outside the relationship to be the
norm, and viewed adopting monogamous standards as an act of oppression.
• In *Male and Female Homosexuality*, M. Saghir and E. Robins found
that the average male homosexual live-in relationship lasts between two
and three years.
• In their *Journal of Sex Research* study of the sexual practices of older
homosexual men, Paul Van de Ven et al. found that only 2.7 percent of
older homosexuals had only one sexual partner in their lifetime.

---

*"The incidence of domestic violence among gay men
is nearly double that in the heterosexual population."*

Comparison of Homosexual 'Couples' and Heterosexual Spouses.
Lest anyone suffer the illusion that any equivalency between the sexual practices of homosexual relationships and traditional marriage exists,
the statistics regarding sexual fidelity within marriage are revealing:
• In *Sex in America*, called by the *New York Times* "the most important
study of American sexual behavior since the Kinsey reports," Robert T.
Michael et al. report that 90 percent of wives and 75 percent of husbands
claim never to have had extramarital sex.
• A nationally representative survey of 884 men and 1,288 women published in *Journal of Sex Research*, found that 77 percent of married men and
88 percent of married women had remained faithful to their marriage vows.
• In *The Social Organization of Sexuality: Sexual Practices in the United
States*, E.O. Laumann et al. conducted a national survey that found that
75 percent of husbands and 85 percent of wives never had sexual relations outside of marriage.
• A telephone survey conducted for *Parade* magazine of 1,049 adults
selected to represent the demographic characteristics of the United States
found that 81 percent of married men and 85 percent of married women
reported that they had never violated their marriage vows.
While the rate of fidelity within marriage cited by these studies re-
mains far from ideal, there is a magnum order of difference between the
negligible lifetime fidelity rate cited for homosexuals and the 75 to 90
percent cited for married couples. This indicates that even "committed"
homosexual relationships display a fundamental incapacity for the faith-
fulness and commitment that is axiomatic to the institution of marriage.

Unhealthy aspects of "monogamous"
homosexual relationships

Even those homosexual relationships that are loosely termed "monogamous" do not necessarily result in healthier behavior.

• The journal *AIDS* reported that men involved in relationships engaged in anal intercourse and oral-anal intercourse with greater frequency than did those without a steady partner. Anal intercourse has been linked with a host of bacterial and parasitical sexually transmitted diseases, including AIDS.

• The exclusivity of the relationship did not diminish the incidence of unhealthy sexual acts, which are commonplace among homosexuals. An English study published in the same issue of *AIDS* concurred, finding that most "unsafe" sex acts among homosexuals occur in steady relationships.

Of paramount concern are the effects of such a lifestyle upon children. Brad Hayton writes:

> Homosexuals . . . model a poor view of marriage to children. They are taught by example and belief that marital relationships are transitory and mostly sexual in nature. Sexual relationships are primarily for pleasure rather than procreation. And they are taught that monogamy in a marriage is not the norm [and] should be discouraged if one wants a good 'marital' relationship.

Violence in Lesbian and Homosexual Relationships.

• A study in the *Journal of Interpersonal Violence* examined conflict and violence in lesbian relationships. The researchers found that 90 percent of the lesbians surveyed had been recipients of one or more acts of verbal aggression from their intimate partners during the year prior to this study, with 31 percent reporting one or more incidents of physical abuse.

• In a survey of 1,099 lesbians, the *Journal of Social Service Research* found that "slightly more than half of the [lesbians] reported that they had been abused by a female lover/partner. The most frequently indicated forms of abuse were verbal/emotional/psychological abuse and combined physical-psychological abuse."

• In their book *Men Who Beat the Men Who Love Them: Battered Gay Men and Domestic Violence*, D. Island and P. Letellier postulate that "the incidence of domestic violence among gay men is nearly double that in the heterosexual population."

Lesbians are three times more likely to abuse alcohol and to suffer from other compulsive behaviors.

Rate of Intimate Partner Violence Within Marriage.

A little-reported fact is that homosexual and lesbian relationships are far more violent than are traditional married households:

• The Bureau of Justice Statistics (U.S. Department of Justice) reports that married women in traditional families experience the lowest rate of violence compared with women in other types of relationships.

• A report by the Medical Institute for Sexual Health concurred:

> It should be noted that most studies of family violence do not differentiate between married and unmarried partner status. Studies that do make these distinctions have found

that marriage relationships tend to have the least intimate partner violence when compared to cohabiting or dating relationships.

High Incidence of Mental Health Problems Among Homosexuals and Lesbians.
A national survey of lesbians published in the *Journal of Consulting and Clinical Psychology* found that 75 percent of the nearly two-thousand respondents had pursued psychological counseling of some kind, many for treatment of long-term depression or sadness:

> Among the sample as a whole, there was a distressingly high prevalence of life events and behaviors related to mental health problems. Thirty-seven percent had been physically abused and 32 percent had been raped or sexually attacked. Nineteen percent had been involved in incestuous relationships while growing up. Almost one-third used tobacco on a daily basis and about 30 percent drank alcohol more than once a week; 6 percent drank daily. One in five smoked marijuana more than once a month. Twenty-one percent of the sample had thoughts about suicide sometimes or often and 18 percent had actually tried to kill themselves. . . . More than half had felt too nervous to accomplish ordinary activities at some time during the past year and over one-third had been depressed.

Substance Abuse Among Lesbians.
A study published in *Nursing Research* found that lesbians are three times more likely to abuse alcohol and to suffer from other compulsive behaviors:

> Like most problem drinkers, 32 (91 percent) of the participants had abused other drugs as well as alcohol, and many reported compulsive difficulties with food (34 percent), codependency (29 percent), sex (11 percent), and money (6 percent). Forty-six percent had been heavy drinkers with frequent drunkenness.

Greater Risk for Suicide.
• A study of twins that examined the relationship between homosexuality and suicide, published in the *Archives of General Psychiatry*, found that homosexuals with same-sex partners were at greater risk for overall mental health problems, and were 6.5 times more likely than their twins to have attempted suicide. The higher rate was not attributable to mental health or substance abuse disorders.
• Another study published simultaneously in *Archives of General Psychiatry* followed 1007 individuals from birth. Those classified as gay, lesbian, or bisexual were significantly more likely to have had mental health problems. Significantly, in his comments in the same issue of the journal, D. Bailey cautioned against various speculative explanations of the results, such as the view that "widespread prejudice against homosexual people causes them to be unhappy or worse, mentally ill."
Reduced Life Span.
Another factor contributing to the instability of male homosexual

households, which raises the possibility of major disruption for children raised in such households, is the significantly reduced life expectancy of male homosexuals. A study published in the *International Journal of Epidemiology* on the mortality rates of homosexuals concluded:

> In a major Canadian centre, life expectancy at age twenty for gay and bisexual men is eight to twenty years less than for all men. If the same pattern of mortality were to continue, we estimate that nearly half of gay and bisexual men currently aged twenty years will not reach their sixty-fifth birthday. Under even the most liberal assumptions, gay and bisexual men in this urban centre are now experiencing a life expectancy similar to that experienced by all men in Canada in the year 1871.

Concern about children placed in homosexual households who are orphaned because of the destructive homosexual lifestyle is well founded. In 1990, Wayne Tardiff and his partner, Allan Yoder, were the first homosexuals permitted to become adoptive parents in the state of New Jersey. Tardiff died in 1992 at age forty-four; Yoder died a few months later, leaving an orphaned five-year-old.

"Nearly half of gay and bisexual men currently aged twenty years will not reach their sixty-fifth birthday."

Sexual Identity Confusion.
The claim that homosexual households do not "recruit" children into the homosexual lifestyle is refuted by the growing evidence that children raised in such households are more likely to engage in sexual experimentation and in homosexual behavior.

• Studies indicate that 0.3 percent of adult females report having practiced homosexual behavior in the past year, 0.4 percent have practiced homosexual behavior in the last five years, and 3 percent have ever practiced homosexual behavior in their lifetime. A study in *Developmental Psychology* found that 12 percent of the children of lesbians became active lesbians themselves, a rate which is at least four times the base rate of lesbianism in the adult female population.

• Numerous studies indicate that while nearly 5 percent of males report having had a homosexual experience sometime in their lives, the number of exclusive homosexuals is considerably less: Between 1 and 2 percent of males report exclusive homosexual behavior over a several-year period. However, J.M. Bailey et al. found that 9 percent of the adult sons of homosexual fathers were homosexual in their adult sexual behavior: "The rate of homosexuality in the sons (9 percent) is several times higher than that suggested by the population-based surveys and is consistent with a degree of father-to-son transmission."

• Even though they attempted to argue otherwise, S. Golombok and F. Tasker's study revealed in its results section a clear connection between being raised in a lesbian family and homosexuality: "With respect to actual involvement in same-gender sexual relationships, there was a significant difference between groups. . . . None of the children from hetero-sexual families had experienced a lesbian or gay relationship." By con-trast, five (29 percent) of the seventeen daughters and one (13 percent) of the eight sons in homosexual families reported having at least one same-sex relationship.

• These findings have most recently been confirmed in a study ap-pearing in the *American Sociological Review.* Authors Judith Stacey and Timothy J. Biblarz alluded to the "political incorrectness" of their finding of higher rates of homosexuality among children raised in homosexual households: "We recognize the political dangers of pointing out that re-cent studies indicate that a higher proportion of children of lesbigay par-ents are themselves apt to engage in homosexual activity."

• Stacey and Biblarz also reported "some fascinating findings on the number of sexual partners children report," that:

> The adolescent and young adult girls raised by lesbian mothers appear to have been more sexually adventurous and less chaste. . . . In other words, once again, children (es-pecially girls) raised by lesbians appear to depart from tradi-tional gender-based norms, while children raised by hetero-sexual mothers appear to conform to them.

Incest in Homosexual Parent Families.
A study in *Adolescence* found:

> A disproportionate percentage—29 percent—of the adult children of homosexual parents had been specifically sub-jected to sexual molestation by that homosexual parent, compared to only 0.6 percent of adult children of heterosex-ual parents having reported sexual relations with their par-ent. . . . Having a homosexual parent(s) appears to increase the risk of incest with a parent by a factor of about 50.

A political agenda: Redefining marriage

It is not the intention of homosexual activists simply to make it possible for homosexuals and lesbians to partake of conventional married life. By their own admission they aim to change the essential character of mar-riage, removing precisely the aspects of fidelity and chastity that promote stability in the relationship and the home:

• Paula Ettelbrick, former legal director of the Lambda Legal Defense and Education Fund, has stated, "Being queer is more than setting up house, sleeping with a person of the same gender, and seeking state ap-proval for doing so. . . . Being queer means pushing the parameters of sex, sexuality, and family, and in the process transforming the very fabric of society."

• According to homosexual writer and activist Michelangelo Signo-rile, the goal of homosexuals is:

> To fight for same-sex marriage and its benefits and then, once granted, redefine the institution of marriage com-pletely, to demand the right to marry not as a way of ad-hering to society's moral codes but rather to debunk a myth

and radically alter an archaic institution. . . . The most subversive action lesbian and gay men can undertake . . . is to transform the notion of "family" entirely.

• Signorile goes so far as to redefine the term monogamy:

For these men the term "monogamy" simply doesn't necessarily mean sexual exclusivity. . . . The term "open relationship" has for a great many gay men come to have one specific definition: A relationship in which the partners have sex on the outside often, put away their resentment and jealousy, and discuss their outside sex with each other, or share sex partners.

• The views of Signorile and Ettelbrick regarding marriage are widespread in the homosexual community. According to the *Mendola Report*, a mere 26 percent of homosexuals believe that commitment is most important in a marriage relationship.

Former homosexual William Aaron explains why even homosexuals involved in "committed" relationships do not practice monogamy:

In the gay life, fidelity is almost impossible. Since part of the compulsion of homosexuality seems to be a need on the part of the homophile to "absorb" masculinity from his sexual partners, he must be constantly on the lookout for [new partners]. Consequently the most successful homophile "marriages" are those where there is an arrangement between the two to have affairs on the side while maintaining the semblance of permanence in their living arrangement.

Even those who support the concept of homosexual "families" admit to their unsuitability for children:

• In their study in *Family Relations*, L. Koepke et al. observed, "Even individuals who believe that same-sex relationships are a legitimate choice for adults may feel that children will suffer from being reared in such families."

• Writing in the *Journal of Homosexuality*, J.J. Bigner and R.B. Jacobson describe the homosexual father as "socioculturally unique," trying to take on "two apparently opposing roles: that of a father (with all its usual connotations) and that of a homosexual man." They describe the homosexual father as "both structurally and psychologically at social odds with his interest in keeping one foot in both worlds: parenting and homosexuality."

Even those who support the concept of homosexual "families" admit to their unsuitability for children.

In truth, the two roles are fundamentally incompatible. The instability, susceptibility to disease, and domestic violence that is disproportionate in homosexual and lesbian relationships would normally render such households unfit to be granted custody of children. However, in the current social imperative to rush headlong into granting legitimacy to the practice of homosexuality in every conceivable area of life, such considerations are often ignored.

But children are not guinea pigs to be used in social experiments in redefining the institution of marriage. They are vulnerable individuals with vital emotional and developmental needs. The great harm done by denying them both a mother and a father in a committed marriage will not easily be reversed, and society will pay a grievous price for its ill-advised adventurism.

Children need a mom and a dad

Attempts to redefine the very nature of the family ignore the accumulated wisdom of cultures and societies from time immemorial, which testifies that the best way for children to be raised is by a mother and father who are married to each other. The importance of the traditional family has been increasingly verified by research showing that children from married two-parent households do better academically, financially, emotionally, and behaviorally. They delay sex longer, have better health, and receive more parental support.

Homosexual or lesbian households are no substitute for a family: Children also need both a mother and a father. David Blankenhorn discusses the different but necessary roles that mothers and fathers play in children's lives: "If mothers are likely to devote special attention to their children's present physical and emotional needs, fathers are likely to devote special attention to their character traits necessary for the future, especially qualities such as independence, self-reliance, and the willingness to test limits and take risks." Blankenhorn further explains:

> Compared to a mother's love, a father's love is frequently more expectant, more instrumental, and significantly less conditional. . . . For the child, from the beginning, the mother's love is an unquestioned source of comfort and the foundation of human attachment. But the father's love is almost a bit farther away, more distant and contingent. Compared to the mother's love, the father's must frequently be sought after, deserved, earned through achievement.

Author and sociologist David Popenoe confirms that mothers and fathers fulfill different roles in their children's lives. In *Life Without Father* Popenoe notes, "Through their play, as well as in their other child-rearing activities, fathers tend to stress competition, challenge, initiative, risk taking and independence. Mothers in their care-taking roles, in contrast, stress emotional security and personal safety." Parents also discipline their children differently: "While mothers provide an important flexibility and sympathy in their discipline, fathers provide ultimate predictability and consistency. Both dimensions are critical for an efficient, balanced, and humane child-rearing regime."

The complementary aspects of parenting that mothers and fathers contribute to the rearing of children are rooted in the innate differences of the two sexes, and can no more be arbitrarily substituted than can the very nature of male and female. Accusations of sexism and homophobia notwithstanding, along with attempts to deny the importance of both mothers and fathers in the rearing of children, the oldest family structure of all turns out to be the best.

A matter of survival

In his analysis of human cultures, the eminent Harvard sociologist Pitirim Sorokin argued that no society has ceased to honor the institution of marriage and survived. Sorokin considered traditional marriage and parenting as the fulfillment of life's meaning for both individuals and society:

> Enjoying the marital union in its infinite richness, parents freely fulfill many other paramount tasks. They maintain the procreation of the human race. Through their progeny they determine the hereditary and acquired characteristics of future generations. Through marriage they achieve a social immortality of their own, of their ancestors, and of their particular groups and community. This immortality is secured through the transmission of their name and values, and of their traditions and ways of life to their children, grandchildren, and later generations.

In the 1981 Apostolic Exhortation *Familiaris Consortio*, Pope John Paul II summarized the importance of marriage-based families:

> The family has vital and organic links with society since it is its foundation and nourishes it continually through its role of service to life: It is from the family that citizens come to birth and it is within the family that they find the first school of the social virtues that are the animating principle of the existence and development of society itself.

None of this is possible in homosexual or lesbian households, which are by definition incapable of creating progeny and contributing to the "procreation of the human race." Any children found in such households are of necessity obtained either from married couples or otherwise through the sexual union of male and female, artificially or otherwise. Thus such households are ironically dependent upon the very womb of society—the union of male and female—that they wish so fervently to deny.

In *It Takes a Village*, Hillary Rodham Clinton refers, perhaps inadvertently, to indelible "laws of nature" when she observes that "every society requires a critical mass of families that fit the traditional ideal." Similarly, an organism needs a critical mass of healthy cells to survive, and—as every oncologist knows—the fewer abnormal cells the better. In a democratic society, those who choose to cohabit in "alternative" familial arrangements such as same-sex unions have the freedom to do so. But toleration is one thing; promotion and "celebration" are another. To entrust children to such arrangements is wholly beyond the pale. As history shows, a society that champions such unions at the expense of traditional families does so at its own peril. But with the formidable forces of nature, culture, and history arrayed against them, such efforts to remake the most fundamental institution of society are not likely, in the end, to prevail.

4

Gay Parenting Does Not Place Children at Risk

American Civil Liberties Union

The American Civil Liberties Union is a national organization that works to defend civil rights guaranteed by the U.S. Constitution.

Recognizing that gays and lesbians can be good parents, the majority of states in America protect the civil rights of gay and lesbian families. Research shows that children of gay and lesbian parents develop as successfully as those of heterosexual parents. Despite the evidence, some adoption and foster care agencies do not accept homosexual applicants, leaving too many children without families. Misperceptions about gay and lesbian parents must be corrected so more children can benefit from the love and care of gay and lesbian parents.

The last decade has seen a sharp rise in the number of lesbians and gay men forming their own families through adoption, foster care, artificial insemination and other means. Researchers estimate that the total number of children nationwide living with at least one gay parent ranges from six to 14 million.

At the same time, the United States is facing a critical shortage of adoptive and foster parents. As a result, hundreds of thousands of children in this country are without permanent homes. These children languish for months, even years, within state foster care systems that lack qualified foster parents and are frequently riddled with other problems. In Arkansas, for example, the foster care system does such a poor job of caring for children that it has been placed under court supervision.

Legal and policy overview of lesbian and gay parenting

Many states have moved to safeguard the interests of children with gay or lesbian parents. For example, at least 21 states have granted second-parent adoptions to lesbian and gay couples, ensuring that their children can enjoy the benefits of having two legal parents, especially if one of the parents dies or becomes incapacitated.

American Civil Liberties Union, "ACLU Fact Sheet: Overview of Lesbian and Gay Parenting, Adoption, and Foster Care," www.aclu.org, April 6, 1999. Copyright © 1999 by the American Civil Liberties Union. Reproduced by permission.

Recognizing that lesbians and gay men can be good parents, the vast majority of states no longer deny custody or visitation to a person based on sexual orientation. State agencies and courts now apply a "best interest of the child" standard to decide these cases. Under this approach, a person's sexual orientation cannot be the basis for ending or limiting parent-child relationships unless it is demonstrated that it causes harm to a child—a claim that has been routinely disproved by social science research. Using this standard, more than 22 states to date have allowed lesbians and gay men to adopt children either through state-run or private adoption agencies.

Nonetheless, a few states—relying on myths and stereotypes—have used a parent's sexual orientation to deny custody, adoption, visitation and foster care. For instance, two states (Florida and New Hampshire) have laws that expressly bar lesbians and gay men from ever adopting children. In a notorious 1993 decision, a court in Virginia took away Sharon Bottoms' 2-year-old son simply because of her sexual orientation, and transferred custody to the boy's maternal grandmother. And Arkansas has just adopted a policy prohibiting lesbians, gay men, and those who live with them, from serving as foster parents.

Research overview of lesbian and gay parenting

All of the research to date has reached the same unequivocal conclusion about gay parenting: the children of lesbian and gay parents grow up as successfully as the children of heterosexual parents. In fact, not a single study has found the children of lesbian or gay parents to be disadvantaged because of their parents' sexual orientation. Other key findings include:

• There is no evidence to suggest that lesbians and gay men are unfit to be parents.

• Home environments with lesbian and gay parents are as likely to successfully support a child's development as those with heterosexual parents.

• Good parenting is not influenced by sexual orientation. Rather, it is influenced most profoundly by a parent's ability to create a loving and nurturing home—an ability that does not depend on whether a parent is gay or straight.

• There is no evidence to suggest that the children of lesbian and gay parents are less intelligent, suffer from more problems, are less popular, or have lower self-esteem than children of heterosexual parents.

• The children of lesbian and gay parents grow up as happy, healthy and well-adjusted as the children of heterosexual parents.

A crisis in adoption and foster care

Right now there is a critical shortage of adoptive and foster parents in the United States. As a result, many children have no permanent homes, while others are forced to survive in an endless series of substandard foster homes. It is estimated that there are 500,000 children in foster care nationally, and 100,000 need to be adopted. But [in 1998] there were qualified adoptive parents available for only 20,000 of these children. Many of these children have historically been viewed as "unadoptable" because they are not healthy white infants. Instead, they are often minority children and/or adolescents, many with significant health problems.

There is much evidence documenting the serious damage suffered by children without permanent homes who are placed in substandard foster homes. Children frequently become victims of the "foster care shuffle," in which they are moved from temporary home to temporary home. A child stuck in permanent foster care can live in 20 or more homes by the time she reaches 18. It is not surprising, therefore, that long-term foster care is associated with increased emotional problems, delinquency, substance abuse and academic problems.

As a result of the increased inclusiveness of modern adoption and foster care policies, thousands of children now have homes with qualified parents.

In order to reach out and find more and better parents for children without homes, adoption and foster care policies have become increasingly inclusive over the past two decades. While adoption and foster care were once viewed as services offered to infertile, middle-class, largely white couples seeking healthy same-race infants, these policies have modernized. In the past two decades, child welfare agencies have changed their policies to make adoption and foster care possible for a much broader range of adults, including minority families, older individuals, families who already have children, single parents (male and female), individuals with physical disabilities, and families across a broad economic range. These changes have often been controversial at the outset. According to the CWLA [Child Welfare League of America], "at one time or another, the inclusion of each of these groups has caused controversy. Many well-intended individuals vigorously opposed including each new group as potential adopters and voiced concern that standards were being lowered in a way that could forever damage the field of adoption."

As a result of the increased inclusiveness of modern adoption and foster care policies, thousands of children now have homes with qualified parents.

Myths vs. facts

Myth: The only acceptable home for a child is one with a mother and father who are married to each other.

Fact: Children without homes do not have the option of choosing between a married mother and father or some other type of parent(s). These children have neither a mother nor a father, married or unmarried. There simply are not enough married mothers and fathers who are interested in adoption and foster care. Last year only 20,000 of the 100,000 foster children in need of adoption were adopted, including children adopted by single people as well as married couples. Our adoption and foster care policies must deal with reality, or these children will never have stable and loving homes.

Myth: Children need a mother and a father to have proper male and female role models.

Fact: Children without homes have neither a mother nor a father as role models. And children get their role models from many places besides their parents. These include grandparents, aunts and uncles, teachers, friends, and neighbors. In a case-by-case evaluation, trained professionals can ensure that the child to be adopted or placed in foster care is moving into an environment with adequate role models of all types.

All of the evidence shows that lesbians and gay men can and do make good parents.

Myth: Gays and lesbians don't have stable relationships and don't know how to be good parents.

Fact: Like other adults in this country, the majority of lesbians and gay men are in stable committed relationships. Of course some of these relationships have problems, as do some heterosexual relationships. The adoption and foster care screening process is very rigorous, including extensive home visits and interviews of prospective parents. It is designed to screen out those individuals who are not qualified to adopt or be foster parents, for whatever reason. All of the evidence shows that lesbians and gay men can and do make good parents. The American Psychological Association, in a recent report reviewing the research, observed that "not a single study has found children of gay or lesbian parents to be disadvantaged in any significant respect relative to children of heterosexual parents," and concluded that "home environments provided by gay and lesbian parents are as likely as those provided by heterosexual parents to support and enable children's psychosocial growth." That is why the Child Welfare League of America, the nation's oldest children's advocacy organization, and the North American Council on Adoptable Children say that gays and lesbians seeking to adopt should be evaluated just like other adoptive applicants.

Myth: Children raised by gay or lesbian parents are more likely to grow up gay themselves.

Fact: All of the available evidence demonstrates that the sexual orientation of parents has no impact on the sexual orientation of their children and that children of lesbian and gay parents are no more likely than any other child to grow up to be gay. There is some evidence that children of gays and lesbians are more tolerant of diversity, but this is certainly not a disadvantage. Of course, some children of lesbians and gay men will grow up to be gay, as will some children of heterosexual parents. These children will have the added advantage of being raised by parents who are supportive and accepting in a world that can sometimes be hostile.

Myth: Children who are raised by lesbian or gay parents will be subjected to harassment and will be rejected by their peers.

Fact: Children make fun of other children for all kinds of reasons: for being too short or too tall, for being too thin or too fat, for being of a different race or religion or speaking a different language. Children show remarkable resiliency, especially if they are provided with a stable and loving home environment. Children in foster care can face tremendous abuse from their peers for being parentless. These children often internalize that abuse, and often feel unwanted. Unfortunately, they do not have the emotional support of a loving permanent family to help them through these difficult times.

Myth: Lesbians and gay men are more likely to molest children.

Fact: There is no connection between homosexuality and pedophilia. All of the legitimate scientific evidence shows that. Sexual orientation, whether heterosexual or homosexual, is an adult sexual attraction to others. Pedophilia, on the other hand, is an adult sexual attraction to children. Ninety percent of child abuse is committed by heterosexual men. In one study of 269 cases of child sexual abuse, only two offenders were gay or lesbian. Of the cases studied involving molestation of a boy by a man, 74 percent of the men were or had been in a heterosexual relationship with the boy's mother or another female relative. The study concluded that "a child's risk of being molested by his or her relative's heterosexual partner is over 100 times greater than by someone who might be identifiable as being homosexual, lesbian, or bisexual."

Myth: Children raised by lesbians and gay men will be brought up in an "immoral" environment.

Fact: There are all kinds of disagreements in this country about what is moral and what is immoral. Some people may think raising children without religion is immoral, yet atheists are allowed to adopt and be foster parents. Some people think drinking and gambling are immoral, but these things don't disqualify someone from being evaluated as an adoptive or foster parent. If we eliminated all of the people who could possibly be considered "immoral," we would have almost no parents left to adopt and provide foster care. That can't be the right solution. What we can probably all agree on is that it is immoral to leave children without homes when there are qualified parents waiting to raise them. And that is what many gays and lesbians can do.

5

Gay Adoption Is Commonly Accepted

Evan B. Donaldson Adoption Institute

The Evan B. Donaldson Adoption Institute seeks to improve adoption through innovative programs, educational initiatives, research and analysis, and advocacy for better practices, policies, and laws.

A systematic, nationwide survey of representative adoption agencies clearly shows that a solid majority are accepting applications from self-identified gays and lesbians. Moreover, many agencies are placing children with gay and lesbian parents on a consistent basis. While some religiously affiliated adoption agencies shun homosexual applicants, others such as Lutheran and Jewish agencies are more likely to place a child with a gay or lesbian client. Public, international, and secular private agencies were also more likely to place children with lesbians or gays. In contrast to much public perception, many children are moving into permanent, loving gay and lesbian households.

Considerable controversy surrounds the issue of parenting by gays and lesbians, and it seems certain to escalate. It is a critical component of the debate over whether homosexuals should be permitted to marry, and it continues to divide policymakers in the United States—as well as in Canada and other countries—as they formulate laws and practices relating to workplace benefits, foster care, adoption, and an array of other important social and personal questions.

Even as these discussions proliferate on the legislative and rhetorical levels, however, reality on the ground is outstripping the pace of the debate. That is, a growing number of lesbians and gay men are becoming parents and are living as families every day, irrespective of what the policymakers do or say.

They are becoming mothers and fathers in many ways, but primarily through insemination, surrogacy and adoption. The latter alternative, which is becoming increasingly popular (though that fact is not generally publicized), provides critical insights into the cultural changes taking place in two major ways: demonstrating that the adoption of children by homosexuals is an ongoing, unabated practice; and showing that Americans' attitudes are evolving—as reflected in the fact that more and more agencies are allowing openly gay and lesbian clients to adopt.

Responding to the need for research

Solid research, to help inform and shape the dialogue, has been lacking. There have been studies, for example, finding that homosexuals' parenting capacity and their children's outcomes are comparable to those of heterosexuals. But little is known about two pivotal aspects of the process: What are adoption agency policies and practices toward prospective adoptive parents who are gay or lesbian? And to what extent are agencies placing children with homosexuals?

In an attempt to address these issues and to promote a more informed dialogue on this topic, the Evan B. Donaldson Adoption Institute—funded by a generous grant from the Rainbow Endowment—conducted a systematic, nationwide analysis of whether agencies work with lesbian and gay prospective adoptive parents, the extent to which agencies place children with them, and agency staff attitudes regarding adoption by homosexuals.

A clear majority of all responding agencies (60%) said they accepted applications from self-identified lesbians and gays in 1999–2000.

The most sweeping conclusion that comes out of the research is simply that adoption agencies are increasingly willing to place children with gay and lesbian adults and, consequently, a steadily escalating number of homosexuals are becoming adoptive parents.

Among the study's principal specific findings are:

• Lesbians and gays are adopting regularly, in notable and growing numbers, at both public and private agencies nationwide.

• Assuming those responding are representative (and the results show they are), 60% of adoption agencies accept applications from homosexuals.

• About 2 in 5 of all agencies in the country have placed children with adoptive parents whom they know to be gay or lesbian.

• Most likely to place children with homosexuals are public, secular private, Jewish- and Lutheran-affiliated agencies, and those focusing on special needs and international adoption.

In addition to the specific findings, the study's results lead to several major conclusions on the levels of policy and practice:

• For lesbians and gay men, the opportunities for becoming adoptive mothers and fathers is significantly greater than is generally portrayed in the media or perceived by the public.

• Though a large and growing number of agencies work with or are willing to work with homosexual clients, they often are unsure about whether or how to reach out to them.

• Because so many homosexuals are becoming adoptive parents, it is important for the sake of their children that agencies develop pre-placement and post-placement services.

Surveys requesting information about agency policies and practices in 1999–2000 were mailed to adoption program directors at all 51 public agencies in the United States, plus 844 private agencies (over half of all those listed in the National Adoption Information Clearinghouse database, randomly chosen within each state). Of those, 307 adoption agencies responded—277 private and 30 public—representing a statistically strong 41% response rate (eliminating surveys returned as undeliverable, and from agencies not making adoption placements). The margin of error is plus or minus 5%. As a whole, about one-third of the agencies focused primarily on domestic infant/toddler adoptions and one-third on special needs adoptions. International adoptions were provided by approximately one-fifth of the agencies and one-tenth had mixed adoption programs. About half of the private agencies (177) did not have a religious affiliation, while the rest represented a variety of faiths.

Research results: More adoption by homosexuals

In general, the study's results confirm that adoptions by lesbians and gays are occurring regularly and in notable numbers, both at public and private agencies. The research also reveals that the acceptance of applications from homosexual clients, as well as the placement of children with lesbians and gays, is associated with both program type (special needs, private domestic infant, international) and religious affiliation or non-affiliation.

A clear majority of all responding agencies (60%) said they accepted applications from self-identified lesbians and gays in 1999–2000. Acceptance of such applications was associated with the agency's type of placement program, with special needs agencies much more likely to accept applications from homosexuals than all other agency types. The vast majority of special needs programs (85.3%) and about two-thirds of international (68.2%) and mixed programs (65.7%) accepted applications from lesbians and gays, while almost half of domestic infant/toddler programs (48%) accepted such applications.

Adoptive placements of children with lesbians and gays varied as a function of program type and religious affiliation.

There was also a significant difference in the acceptance of adoption applications from homosexuals as a function of the agency's religious affiliation. Jewish-affiliated agencies were universally willing to work with gay and lesbian clients, as were the vast majority of public agencies (90%), private agencies with no religious affiliation (80.2%), and most Lutheran agencies (66.7%). The rest of the agencies were much less willing to accept applications from homosexuals, although a sizable minority of Methodist and Catholic agencies did. About 20% of all agencies said that, on one or more occasions, they had rejected applications from homosexual prospective adoptive parents.

Almost two-thirds of responding agencies had official policies on adoption by gays and lesbians; of those, 33.6% reported a non-discrimination policy. About one-fifth responded that placement decisions were guided by the children's country of origin, and another fifth said that religious beliefs were the basis for rejecting applications from homosexuals. Significantly, of the agencies choosing not to participate in the survey, more than one-third reported in follow-up phone calls that they did not work with homosexual prospective adoptive parents.

Placing children with lesbian and gay parents

About 2 in 5 (39%) of all agencies had placed at least one child with a homosexual adoptive parent in 1999–2000. Because many of these agencies did not keep such statistics—fewer than half (43%) collected information on prospective adoptive parents' sexual orientation—and since it was impossible to estimate the number of such placements they made, only one adoption placement with a homosexual client per year was counted for statistical purposes. Based on this conservative approach, respondents made a total of 1,206 such placements, or 1.3% of their total placements, though it's apparent that the true number must be appreciably higher.

As with the acceptance of applications, adoptive placements of children with lesbians and gays varied as a function of program type and religious affiliation. The majority of special needs (61.5%) and international agencies (51.5%) made placements with homosexual clients. In contrast, fewer than half of the agencies with mixed adoption programs (45.7%) and only a quarter of agencies focusing on domestic infant adoptions (25.5%) made such placements. Public agencies (83.3%), Jewish-affiliated agencies (73.7%), private, secular agencies (55.9%) and Lutheran agencies (53.3%) were significantly more likely to make an adoption placement with a homosexual client than all other types of agencies.

As for informing potential birth parents when making an adoptive placement with lesbian or gay individuals, almost half of the respondents (47%) provided that information as a matter of policy or routine practice. A larger percentage (76.9%) of domestic infant agencies, than special needs and international programs, provided the information to prospective birth parents because the latter agencies have little contact with the child's biological parents during the adoption planning process.

On related issues, the Adoption Institute research found:

• About one-quarter of respondents said prospective birth parents have objected to placing their child with gays or lesbians, or have specifically requested their child not be placed with homosexuals. At the same time, nearly 15% of all agencies said birth parents had requested or chosen lesbian or gay prospective adoptive parents for their child on at least one occasion.

• Though most agencies worked with lesbians and gays, only 19% sought them to be adoptive parents and the vast majority of these (86.6%) relied on word of mouth for recruitment. Outreach efforts were made most often at agencies already willing to work with homosexuals (41.7% of Jewish affiliated, 29.9% of private, non-religiously affiliated, and 20% of public).

• Similarly, adoption agencies focused on children with special needs were the most likely to make outreach efforts (32.1%) to gays and lesbians, followed by international focused agencies (19.7%).

• Nearly half (48%) indicated an interest in receiving training to work with lesbian and gay prospective parents. Most likely to be interested were agencies already working with them: public, non-religiously affiliated, Jewish and Lutheran. Additionally, special needs programs and those with mixed programs were more likely to be interested in training than were those focusing on international and domestic infant adoptions.

Adoption directors' personal attitudes also were associated with the agency's religious affiliations and program types. Directors of agencies focusing on domestic infant adoption were significantly less likely to be accepting of homosexual adoption compared to respondents from other agencies. They also were more likely to believe homosexual clients need greater evaluation, preparation, and/or support when adopting than were adoption directors at agencies focused on special needs or international placements. Respondents from public and non-religiously affiliated private agencies, as well as Jewish agencies, were more accepting of gay and lesbian adoption and less likely to believe that homosexuals needed more intensive evaluation, preparation, and support when adopting a child.

Directors who scored higher on the "acceptance of homosexual adoption" variable, and lower on the "need for greater evaluation and support" variable, worked in agencies that more often accepted adoption applications from lesbians and gays, were more likely to have made a placement with this group, were more likely to have recruited gays and lesbians as prospective applicants, and expressed more desire for training in relation to homosexual adoption.

The study's findings offer insights into a controversial arena of adoption, as well as into an important issue in the gay and lesbian community. For society, the bottom line is clear: Homosexuals are becoming parents in growing numbers, and adoption agencies are fueling the trend. For homosexuals wishing to become parents, the results paint a more encouraging picture than is often portrayed or perceived by many (if not most) Americans. Although stereotypes and misconceptions still perpetuate policy and practice, from a child-centered perspective, the willingness of adoption agencies to accept gay and lesbian adults as parents means more and more waiting children are moving into permanent, loving families.

6

Gay Adoption Should Not Be Accepted

Paul Cameron

Paul Cameron is chairman of the conservative Family Research Institute in Colorado Springs, Colorado.

Professional organizations, such as the American Academy of Pediatrics, have come out in support of adoption by gay and lesbian parents. Unfortunately, the data they use to justify and even praise homosexual parenting is selective and biased. A survey of neglected clinical reports, personal testimony from children reared by gay parents, and comparative studies show that homosexual parenting tends to harm children rather than benefit them. Moreover, due to the shorter life expectancy of homosexuals, children of gay parents are more likely to lose a parent to death. The reports used to support adoption by gay and lesbian parents need to be scrutinized and corrected.

On Feb. 4, 2000, the American Academy of Pediatrics (AAP) recommended "legal and legislative efforts" to allow children "born to or adopted by one member of a gay or lesbian couple" to be adopted by the homosexual partner. Such a law effectively would eliminate the possibility of adoption by other family members following the death of the parent. It also would cause problems for numerous children.

The AAP, like many other professional organizations, apparently was too caught up in promoting identity politics to address all the evidence relevant to homosexual adoption. In its report, the organization offered only positive evidence about gays and lesbians as parents. "In fact," the report concluded, "growing up with parents who are lesbian or gay may confer some advantages to children." Really?

There are three sets of information on the issue: clinical reports of psychiatric disturbance of children with homosexual parents, testimonies of children with homosexual parents concerning their situation and studies that have compared the children of homosexuals with the children of nonhomosexuals. The AAP ignored the first two sets and had to cherry-

51

pick the comparative studies to arrive at the claim that "no data have pointed to any risk to children as a result of growing up in a family with one or more gay parents."

Neglected clinical reports and testimony

A number of clinical reports detail "acting-out behavior," homosexual seduction, elective muteness and the desire for a mother by children with homosexual parents. I am unaware of a single child being disturbed because his mother and father were married.

The AAP also ignored the testimonies of children with homosexual parents—probably the best evidence since these kids had to "live with it" rather than deal with a theory. More than 150 children with homosexual parents have provided, in extensive interviews, detailed evidence of the difficulties they encountered as a result. A study Paul and Kirk Cameron published this year in *Psychological Reports* analyzed the content of 57 life-story narratives by children with homosexual parents assembled by lesbian researchers Louise Rafkin (United States) and Lisa Saffron (Britain).

In these narratives, children in 48 of the 52 families (92 percent) mentioned one or more "problems." Of the 213 problems which were scored—including hypersexuality, instability, molestation, domestic violence—children attributed 201 (94 percent) to their homosexual parent(s).

Here are four sample excerpts:

• One 9-year-old girl said: "My biological mother is S. and my other mother is L. We've lived together for a year. Before that L. lived across the street. . . . My mom met L.; L. had just broken up with someone. We moved in together because it got complicated going back and forth every night. All of a sudden I felt like I was a different person because my mom was a lesbian. . . . I get angry because I can't tell anybody about my mom. The kids at school would laugh. . . . They say awful things about lesbians . . . then they make fun of me. Having lesbian mothers is nothing to laugh about. . . . I have told my [mother] that she has made my life difficult."

• A 12-year-old boy in the United Kingdom said: "Mum . . . has had several girlfriends in my lifetime. . . . I don't go around saying that I've got two mums. . . . If we are sitting in a restaurant eating, she'll say, 'I want you to know about all these sex things.' And she'll go on about everything, just shouting it out. . . . Sometimes when mum embarrasses me, I think, 'I wish I had a dad.' . . . Been to every gay pride march. Last year, while attending, we went up to a field . . . when two men came up to us. One of them started touching me. I didn't want to go this year because of that."

• According to a 39-year-old woman: "In my memories, I'm always looking for my mother and finding her with a woman doing things I don't understand. . . . Sometimes they blame me for opening a door that wasn't even locked. . . . [At about the age of 10], I noticed a door that I hadn't yet opened. Inside I saw a big bed. My mother sat up suddenly and stared at me. She was with B. . . . and then B. shouted, 'You f***ing sneaking brat!' My mother never said a word. [Then came N.] I came to hate N. because of the way she and my mother fought every night. They screamed and bickered and whined and pouted over everything. N. closed my mother's hand in the car door. . . . She and N. hadn't made love in seven years."

• According to a 19-year-old man: "When I was about 7, my mother told me that this woman, D., was going to stay with us for a while—and she never left! I didn't think anything much about it until I was about 10. . . . It just became obvious because she and my mother were sleeping together. A few months after D. left, my mother started to see another woman, but that didn't last. Then she got involved with a different woman . . . ; she'd be violent toward my mother. . . . After that she started to go on marches and to women's groups. . . . There were some women in these groups who objected to men altogether, and I couldn't cope with that."

All 57 narratives can be found at www.familyresearchinst.org. Anyone who believes that living with homosexual parents confers "some advantages to children" should read these accounts.

Neglected comparative studies

The AAP ignored every comparative study of children that showed those with homosexual parents experiencing more problems. These include the largest comparative study, reported in 1996 by Sotirios Sarantakos in the journal, *Children Australia*, of 58 elementary schoolchildren raised by coupled homosexual parents who were closely matched (by age, sex, grade in school, social class) with 58 children of cohabiting heterosexual parents and 58 raised by married parents. Teachers reported that the married couples' children scored best at math and language but somewhat lower in social studies, experienced the highest level of parental involvement at school as well as at home and had parents with the highest expectations for them. The children of homosexuals scored lowest in math and language and somewhat higher in social studies, were the least popular, experienced the lowest level of parental involvement at school and at home, had parents with the lowest expectations for them and least frequently expressed higher educational and career expectations.

Yet the AAP said that studies have "failed to document any differences between such groups on . . . academic success." The organization's report also ignored the only empirical study based upon a random sample that reported on 17 adults (out of a sample of 5,182) with homosexual parents. Detailed by Cameron and Cameron in the journal *Adolescence* in 1996, the 17 were disproportionately apt to report sexual relations with their parents, more apt to report a less than exclusively heterosexual orientation, more frequently reported gender dissatisfaction and were more apt to report that their first sexual experience was homosexual.

The AAP report also seemingly ignored a 1998 *Psychological Reports* study by Cameron and Cameron that included the largest number of children with homosexual parents. That study compared 73 children of homosexuals with 105 children of heterosexuals. Of the 66 problems cited by panels of judges who extensively reviewed the living conditions and psychological reactions of children of homosexuals undergoing a divorce from heterosexuals, 64 (97 percent) were attributed to the homosexual parent.

Finally, while ignoring studies that contradicted its own conclusions, the AAP misrepresented numerous findings from the limited literature it cited. Thus, Sharon Huggins compared 18 children of 16 volunteer/ lesbian mothers with 18 children of 16 volunteer/heterosexual/divorced mothers on self-esteem. Huggins reported statistically nonsignificant differences between the 19 children of mothers who were not living with a lover versus the 17 children of mothers who were living with a lover; and, further, that [the four] "adolescent daughters with high self-esteem had been told of their mother's lesbianism at a mean age of 6.0 years. In contrast, [the five] adolescent daughters with low self-esteem had been told at a mean age of 9.6 years" and "three of four of the mothers with high self-esteem daughters were currently living with lesbian lovers, but only one of four of the lesbian mothers with low self-esteem daughters was currently living with a lesbian lover."

The AAP cited Huggins as proving that "children's self-esteem has been shown to be higher among adolescents whose mothers (of any sexual orientation) were in a new partnered relationship after divorce, compared with those whose mother remained single, and among those who found out at a younger age that their parent was homosexual, compared with those who found out when they were older," thus transforming statistical nonevents based on niggling numbers of volunteers into important differences—twice in one sentence!

Death rates for lesbians and gays

We have examined more than 10,000 obituaries of homosexuals: The median age of death for lesbians was in the 40s to 50s; for homosexuals it was in the 40s. Most Americans live into their 70s. Yet in the 1996 U.S. government sex survey the oldest lesbian was 49 years old and the oldest gay 54.

Children with homosexual parents are considerably more apt to lose a parent to death. Indeed, a homosexual couple in their 30s is roughly equivalent to a nonhomosexual couple in their late 40s or 50s. Adoption agencies will seldom permit a couple in their late 40s or 50s to adopt a child because of the risk of parental death, and the consequent social and psychological difficulty for the child. The AAP did not address this fact—one with profound implications for any child legally related to a homosexual.

As usual, the media picked up on the AAP report as authoritative, assuming that it represented the consensus of a large and highly educated membership. Not so. As in other professional organizations, the vast majority of members pay their dues, read the journal and never engage in professional politics. As a consequence, a small but active minority of members gains control and uses the organization to promote its agenda. Too often, the result is ideological literature that misrepresents the true state of knowledge.

Gay-rights activists have been particularly adept at manipulating research and reports to their own ends. For years the media reported that all studies revealed that 10 percent of the population was homosexual. In fact, few if any studies ever came to that conclusion. For the next few years we will have to live with the repeated generalization that all studies prove homosexual parents are as good for children as heterosexual parents, and perhaps even better. What little literature exists on the subject proves no such thing. Indeed, translated into the language of accounting, the AAP report could be described as "cooking the books."

7

More Gay and Lesbian Teens Are Telling Others They Are Homosexual

Robert E. Owens Jr.

Robert E. Owens Jr. is a professor of communicative disorders at the State University of New York at Geneseo and the author of Queer Kids: The Challenges and Promise for Lesbian, Gay, and Bisexual Youth, *from which this viewpoint was excerpted.*

Recent studies show that more people are self-identifying as gay, lesbian, or bisexual at a younger age and sharing that information with others. The process of declaring sexual identity by "coming out" tends to follow three stages, including coming out to oneself, coming out to friends and family, and living openly as a gay, lesbian, or bisexual person. Telling family members can be a daunting experience for adolescents, and family reactions can vary from absolute support to complete rejection. Parents should be supportive when their teens come out to them.

Coming out of the closet or simple *coming out* or *outing oneself* is a developmental process, a self-affirming rite, through which lesbian, gay, and bisexual individuals first recognize their sexual orientation and develop positive feelings about themselves and that orientation and then integrate this knowledge into their lives. The process has cognitive, affective, and behavioral aspects. It is important to recognize that coming out is a *process*—not an outcome or single event—that occurs every time a lesbian, gay, or bisexual person shares the news of her or his sexuality with another person. With each new acquaintance, the process begins anew.

The act of coming out is as individualistic as the person involved. "On Halloween, all of my close friends and I were gathered in one of our bedrooms counting out loot. . . . I spoke up, 'Hey guys? What would you say if I told you I was gay?' Julia . . . shrugged and said, 'I'd say I was happy for you.' . . . Marion glared, 'Is that all? I've known that since 5th grade!!!'" The extent of coming out is culturally based and the process is not universal.

55

Gay teens

Various studies have found that roughly 40 percent of lesbian and 63 percent of gay adults are open about their sexuality with their parents. Most disclosed to their family members when they were financially independent and living on their own. Some individuals never come out. In contrast to older lesbians, gays, and bisexuals, adolescents are being more open about their sexual orientation and demanding more community support. Most live at home and are not economically self-supporting. The process of disclosure can be perilous.

More and more youths are self-identifying as lesbian, gay, or bisexual at a younger age and remaining open as they get older.

For many, coming out is a "rite of passage" into a well-adjusted adulthood. Although coming out can be social suicide in high school, more and more adolescents view it as a badge of honor or courage and an expression of individuality. In the process, they are increasing the visibility of sexual minorities and making coming out easier for the next teen.

The most frequent reasons given for not self-disclosing are fear of hurt and rejection. Often individuals are afraid that parents will be disappointed or hurt and may reject them. "I want so much for her [her mother] to be proud of me," explains Obie, a young middle-class African-American lesbian,

> I know there are certain things that won't make her proud.
> Being gay is one of them.

In general, young lesbian adults seek support from their families first and then from male and female friends, while young gay men seek support from male friends first and then from families. Fear of peer rejection also exists. Lew's college roommate moved out when he found out about Lew. Glen's basketball buddies stopped asking him to play. Sophie became a pariah in the high school band.

The lesbian and gay communities are so stigmatized that disclosure of same-sex orientation often marks a person as less than whole. Being lesbian or gay typically takes precedence for others over everything else and becomes the entire person.

Who tends to come out?

The demographics on coming out are very interesting. As a group, upper- and middle-class young lesbian and gay adults are more likely than working-class young lesbian and gay adults to be open-about their sexual orientation. Among African Americans, middle-class families, who may be less secure in their status, seem to be less accepting than working-class families of their members who deviate from strict community "norms" or call negative attention to the family. Metropolitan dwellers are more likely to be open than their country and small town cousins. "In a small community," notes 'Lizabeth, a young lesbian, "people here have the ability to make life miserable for you." As a group, men come out before women but women experience fewer mental health problems when coming out and are more open as adults. The difference in age of coming out between men and women may be decreasing. Religiosity seems to be negatively related to self-identification as a male homosexual but not as a lesbian or bisexual. This relationship may reflect the male-centered nature of biblical prohibitions and religious expectations.

In general, those most likely to come out have the lowest levels of homophobia and/or the greatest degree of positive feelings about homosexuality in general. Involvement in sexual-minority political and social organizations and having a supportive environment are positively associated with self-acceptance and coming out. In addition, those most likely to come out have the most comfort with same-sex arousal and lifestyle, more same-sex erotic experiences, a more exclusively homosexual orientation and behavior, and the least fear of negative societal reactions.

By all accounts, more and more youths are self-identifying as lesbian, gay, or bisexual at a younger age and remaining open as they get older. Studies from the early 1970s to the present record a steady decline in the mean age of coming out from nineteen to fifteen or sixteen years of age. Some youth who self-identify early are coming out as early as age fourteen. As a result, the challenges inherent in self-disclosure are now becoming associated with the problems of adolescence.

Coming out is a lifelong process not a one-time event.

No rules exist for coming out, so each individual must improvise. The decision to out oneself is a very personal one in which each person must consider the consequences for herself or himself and for her or his relationships with others. Success in coming out is related in part to the maturity of both the youth and the person to whom she or he is coming out. Coming out is often a disorderly, highly individualized process, characterized by diversions and detours.

Why gay teens decide to come out

The rationale for coming out is simple. Healthy personalities are those that are shared with others. "If I . . . don't tell *anyone*, how long must I keep it all in?" reasons Philip, a gay high schooler with deafness. "What's the point of keeping it in?" "It's been real bad for my parents," confides John. "I just lie to them more and more." Dan, age nineteen, concurs, "Lying is the one thing that I've perfected over the years. . . ." The sexual identification of a person and the social identification that is presented to the world must become consistent or the youth risks feelings of hypocrisy and falsehood that can lead to isolation. Christopher, a young white gay man, explains:

> The hardest part about coming out is telling something that's
> so deep in your heart with the realization that at any point

they could say, "You're immoral; you're wrong.". . . But what's wonderful is that finally you're not lying. You're being completely honest and they're sharing that joy with you.

One of the results of coming out is a decrease in feelings of aloneness and guilt. "I've come out to almost all of my friends," states Michael, age sixteen. "Sometimes it was hell, but nothing compares to holding it inside." Brent, age sixteen, explains further:

I knew my coming out wouldn't allow me to have the same everyday existence heterosexuals did. I knew I'd have more people treating me badly. But at least I wouldn't be treating myself badly. I'd rather be bashed by other people than by myself.

When given an opportunity to renounce his former claim of homosexuality, Joseph Steffan, a high-ranking Annapolis midshipman, refused, responding, "Yes sir, I am." He recalls:

It was a moment I will never forget, one of agony and intense pride. In that one statement, I had given up my dreams, the goals I had spent the last four years of my life laboring to attain. But in exchange, I retained something far more valuable—my honor and my self-esteem.

Common motivations

The benefits of coming out aside, most lesbian and gay individuals come out for reasons other than mental health. Rather, they feel compelled to self-disclose when denial can no longer be sustained, possibly accompanying a relationship or infatuation.

Self-esteem and the degree of openness, especially in a supportive environment, are directly related. More of one leads to more of the other. Those who have been out the longest have the highest self-esteem. Adolescents who have discussed their sexuality with parents feel more confirmed and less anxiety-ridden. Individuals who have come out often report a sense of freedom, of not living a lie, and of genuine acceptance. When Karen first came out in college, she proclaimed, "Finally, for the first time, I felt like who I was."

Being out is also correlated with a positive queer identity. With the fusing of sexuality and emotionality, open homosexuality becomes a preferred way of life.

Although an open lesbian or gay youth may face harassment and hostility, she or he may avoid the negative aspects of nonidentity, including denial, repression, and/or suppression. Aaron Fricke, one of the first adolescents to take a same-sex date to his high school prom, saw his actions as a strong positive statement. He concluded, "I would be showing that my dignity and value as a human being were not affected by my sexual preference." At one level, coming out can be seen as an attempt by the individual to redefine herself or himself rather than to accept the negative societal stereotypes.

Coming out can lead to nonsexual interactions with other lesbians, gays, and bisexuals. The lesbian and gay community can provide support for teens and is a source of friendship, romantic relations, role models, and social norms. In general, it's more important to have someone to talk to than someone to socialize with. The extent of this interaction varies with an individual's social and vocational needs and with the availability of other individuals. Marshall and a friend made frequent trips of several hours length to a large city to explore gay bookstores and to attend gay film festivals and pride marches. Many lesbian, gay, and bisexual youth speak of the exhilaration of attending their first pride or rights march.

Recent studies have found a mean age of sixteen for first disclosure.

In general, coming out can be discussed as a three-step process of coming out to one's self, to others, and to all or "going public." Individuals will vary in the degree of disclosure and degree to which each considers herself or himself to be out. The degree of disclosure will vary with income, occupation, place of habitation, and the sexual orientation of one's friends. At each stage of coming out, the act of disclosure redefines an individual's notion of self which, in turn, influences the process of disclosure.

Although more information is available on lesbians and gays, anecdotal data suggest that the process for bisexuals is similar to that for homosexuals. Gillian came out while driving around with his friend Josh.

> I said "Josh, I really need to talk to you about something. I think I might be bisexual. . . ." And he . . . turns to me and goes "I'm so glad you brought this up because I know that I'm gay. . . ." We gave each other the biggest hug for a long time, just because we knew we were there for each other.

As mentioned, coming out is a lifelong process not a one-time event. We can describe this process in three stages. Their importance for the individual, the difficulty or ease of each, and their length will vary across individuals.

Coming out to self

Coming out to one's self is part of becoming lesbian, gay, or bisexual. An individual passes from nonrecognition through a sense of difference to self-recognition and lesbian, gay, or bisexual affirmation. Feeling different and the growing awareness of what that difference means can create inner tension and affect self-esteem. The realization can be frightening. "I said it to myself when I was fourteen, but I know that I clearly knew it before then; I just didn't admit it to myself," explains a young gay man: "I said to myself, 'I can't be.' I couldn't accept it." Nonetheless, realization can provide a self-explanation and a context for self-examination.

Self-recognition and identity formation are based on more than the emergence of sexual feelings. Lesbian and gay teens and young adults cite other events that contribute to their self-realization. For males, contact with other gay males or with lesbians is particularly important for self-realization. For females, falling in love is the most important event although contact with other lesbians and gay males is a strong second. "I realized that these women were feeling the same things that I felt," recalls a seventeen-year-old lesbian, "and what I'd been reading about lesbians was, in fact, what I am. That's when I started feeling really good."

Self-acceptance and self-esteem are positively related. In general, openness increases and/or is encouraged by self-esteem. Recalling his ordeal at Annapolis after coming out, exmidshipman Joseph Steffan stated, "By coming out to myself, I gained the strength that can come only from self-acceptance, and it was with that added strength that I had been able to persevere. . . . "

Gender differences exist in self-labeling. Males define themselves as gay in the context of same-sex erotic behavior. In contrast, lesbians self-define in the context of romantic love and attachment. In addition, self-labeling appears to be more threatening to males than to females.

Healthy self-esteem is difficult for queer kids to attain in the face of society's negative messages. "I believed all the [negative] things I'd been told," recalls Robin, a sixteen-year-old lesbian. "So I hid from myself." Pervasive negative feelings may make it difficult for a youth to feel good about anything she or he accomplishes. The attitude may become, "Yeah, I won the bowling trophy [received the scholarship, got straight A's, became an Eagle Scout, etc.] but I'm still a faggot [dyke, lezzie, queer, etc.]." With gay-positive feelings self-esteem is enhanced in other areas of life.

Usually, in this phase, sexual orientation is placed in perspective with personal identity so that the stereotypes of lesbians, gays, and bisexuals do not overwhelm other aspects of personality. Sexual orientation becomes only one aspect of the person.

Coming out to others

Disclosure to others is best when the discloser has a strong self-image. Unnecessarily painful disclosure may result if a youth comes out while internalized homophobia is strong and issues of self-worth still unresolved. Christopher, age nineteen, tried to resolve these issues prior to coming out. It took him four years of dealing with his own internalized homophobia before he was ready. "Our society is so homophobic that it can take someone who is gay years before being able to say the words out loud."

Initially, lesbians and gays are very cautious in selecting to whom and when to come out. The relationship with the other person and the expected reaction are considered carefully. Those who are generally supportive of an individual youth and can be described as warm, accepting, and nurturant are the most likely candidates.

Recent studies have found a mean age of sixteen for first disclosure. As a group, lesbian, gay, and bisexual teens usually self-disclose first to a friend, same-sex peer, sibling, or another lesbian or gay teen. Queer kids risk less by telling friends rather than parents. Friends can reject an outed teen, but parents can withdraw financial support. Reportedly, most peers and friends respond favorably, possibly reflecting the selection of tolerant or homosexual confidants. The even more positive responses reported in more current studies may reflect changing attitudes.

Over half of lesbian and gay teens consider their gay friends more important than their families. Of the remainder, 15 percent consider their families more important. Terry, a gay teen, couldn't have wished for a response as positive as his sister's.

> Well, I have a friend who is that way. She's my best friend. I just want to let you know that if you need any help or need to talk, just come to me.

Among parents, mothers usually are informed before fathers, possibly because they are perceived as the more accepting parent. When Jim told his mother, her initial response was to cry and to curse and ridicule him. She later relented and became more accepting. When Marcus, age eighteen, told his father he was gay, his father's response shocked him:

> This isn't what I wish for you. It's not going to be an easy life for you. But I don't love you any less than if you were straight.

Coming out to all

Disclosure to others is an important step in positive self-identification. An individual slowly becomes fully aware of herself or himself as that self is revealed fully to others. Through the coming-out process, lesbian and gay youths develop a sense of self-control and self-respect and begin to heal from the burden of carrying a secret. Without this openness, "the lie" can distort all relationships. The wall that protects the deception results in the youth's isolation. Distancing from others, including parents, becomes a survival technique.

One of the results of being an invisible minority of closeted individuals is that it is difficult for lesbian, gay, and bisexual teens to meet each other. Slowly, in part because of the insistence of these teens themselves, a network of support groups and services is being established.

Those youth who successfully come out usually disclose themselves slowly to others considered to be safe and gradually build a support network. Coming out is a more positive experience if an adolescent gains support from family and friends. Quality of supporters is more important than number of supporters for sixteen- to twenty-year-olds. Those supporters with whom a youth can talk honestly are the most important.

Those young gay men who are out tend to be involved in more gay activities; to be more open about their sexual identity and in a more supportive environment; to describe themselves as accomplished, outgoing, and understanding of the feelings of others; older; better educated; earlier maturing; and from wealthier, more urban families. In contrast, young out lesbian adults are more involved in lesbian and gay rights; have more lesbian and gay friends and family support; and have fewer, if any, sexual relations with men than do closeted lesbians.

Family dynamics

Coming out is not without risk, but the eventual results far outweigh the destructive psychological price of concealment. The most frequent reasons for not coming out are fear of hurting or disappointing loved ones and fear of rejection. Family relationships are a major concern for teens. Disapproval and rejection are very possible reactions. The threat of expulsion from the home is all too real.

Although difficult, coming out to family members is extremely important for identity development. Disclosure to parents, probably one of life's most fearful events, is accompanied by stress and anxiety, especially for a disclosing youth. More than half of lesbian, gay, and bisexual teens and young adults fear disclosing their sexual orientation to their families. "I haven't come out yet to my parents," confesses a young African-American lesbian. "I'm sure it'll be a problem when I do."

Families, the primary socialization context in our society, are awash in heterosexism.

Families, the primary socialization context in our society, are awash in heterosexism. Barbara, the mother of a gay son admits, "You realize that you have expectations for your children that you didn't know you had." Thus, lesbian and gay youth often hide their sexuality from their parents and endure a litany of questions about dating and prospective boyfriends and girlfriends. The secretiveness comes at a cost as noted in the comments of an eighteen-year-old lesbian:

> I was so frustrated from hiding that I just told her [her mother]. . . . But at that point I didn't care anymore.

Not to come out is to surrender to fear and mistrust, to become alienated, and to stifle openness and spontaneity. For some teens, running away is easier than continued deception.

Occasionally, parents will ask about sexual orientation before the youth is ready to come out and before the family and the teen are adequately prepared to discuss the issue maturely and calmly. Beth's mother asked her one Saturday while in the car. Luckily for Beth, her mother was very supportive. Julio's father quizzed him angrily and made verbal threats, but his mother was more reasonable, although she was also very upset.

Matt, an openly gay student in Newton, Massachusetts and three-time state gymnastics champion, was asked by his parents if he was gay when he was fourteen. Initially unsure, Matt had come out to the entire high school by his senior year and was organizing awareness training for students and faculty.

Some parents may not wish to know about their child's sexual orientation. Jacob, an African-American high schooler explains,

> Maybe they were afraid of me saying, "yes." I think that may have been why my parents never mentioned it to me.

Confronting sexual issues may be too difficult for some parents.

The process of telling family members

The coming-out process will vary with the particular family member and the individual lesbian or gay youth. Coming out to the family is especially difficult for males. Siblings are perceived as potentially more accepting than parents. Elderly parents seem to be more negative than younger ones.

In general, more lesbian and gay youths are out to their parents than to other family members with mothers favored over fathers by a ratio of two to one. Mothers often serve a supportive role and negotiate relationships between their lesbian or gay child and other family members.

Travis came out to his mother as a high school junior but feared telling his stepfather, "who doesn't drink homogenized milk because it says 'homo' on the label!" More youth may come out to their mothers because they rightly predict that mothers tend to respond more positively than fathers, who if not negative may just be very nonresponsive. Chris's father pronounced his son's coming out a death sentence. The boyfriend of Thomas's mother scrawled "FAGGOT MAGGOTS" on Thomas's bedroom wall. Mitch's father saw no need for his son to cause "problems" by telling everyone. Vince's father, a very religious man, told his son that he really believed Vince had no choice in his sexual orientation, then explained, "Your orientation is the result of some form of demonic possession."

Young lesbian adults tend to tell siblings earlier and fathers later than do young gay men. Often, the concerns and responses of siblings differ from those of parents. The shame and guilt that parents generally experience is replaced by feelings of embarrassment and betrayal. Siblings may feel that the stigma of homosexuality affects them in some way too.

For a youth to come out may be to risk losing the extended family and bringing disgrace to all its members.

Girls tend to be more open with either parent than boys. Although parental response does not seem to vary with the gender of the child, fathers seem to experience more difficulty accepting the news from their daughters, possibly because lesbian youth seem to be less influenced by prevailing gender roles than males. According to Jennifer, her father "insisted that I was just being rebellious and trying to make him look like a bad father." The greater openness of girls may reflect the more open conversational style of females in general or the less negative societal reaction to lesbians than to gay men. Overall, males receive more negative reactions from their families than do females. In addition, lesbians are more likely than men to view coming out as a political statement.

Negative reactions to coming out

Approximately half of lesbian and gay youth report that they have lost friends or received negative reactions from family members. "I have no friends that are guys," admits Mike, a white nineteen-year-old. Athletic and energetic, he likes football but has no friends with which to play. "They can't get past 'Mike the faggot'," he explains. "I went from very popular to not having any friends," declares Alessandra. "Most people wouldn't talk *to* me but there was a lot of talk behind my back."

Angela's mother found out about her teenage daughter's sexual orientation from reading Angela's diary. Angela now lives alone and is isolated from family members. Scott's parents, who are Jehovah's Witnesses, physically removed him from their home when he came out at age seventeen. No member of his former congregation, including his family, may interact with him.

The response of family members is influenced by such factors as conformity, religion, politics, ethnicity and race, discomfort with sexual matters, and attitudes about family cohesion. Families that emphasize religion, marriage, and children are perceived by lesbian and gay teens as being disappointed at hearing a member's disclosure, although these types of beliefs do not seem to be a factor in whether or not to come out.

Homophobia seems to be more prevalent in ethnic-minority communities, making coming out very difficult. For a youth to come out may be to risk losing the extended family and bringing disgrace to all its members. Losing family support leaves a youth alone, jeopardizing her or his sense of self.

It may be especially difficult to be open in the ethnic-minority community. Even parents who know a child's sexual orientation may not wish to embarrass the family or community by asking. The subject may be quarantined, a taboo topic, especially in Asian-American and Latino homes where sex is discussed rarely, if at all. In these two ethnic communities, approximately 80 percent of lesbian and gay young adults are out to a sister rather than to a parent.

Dealing with preconceptions and expectations

Sex role expectations vary with culture also. In Latino culture, for example, males are expected to exude *machismo*. In contrast, gay men are expected to be effeminate and passive, a *maricón*. Many gay men are not willing to take this "female" role. Lesbians who do not subscribe to this inferior role may be just as subversive. "Being a lesbian is by definition an act of treason against our cultural values," states a Latina lesbian. Gay men who accept the Latino stereotype and lesbians who reject the Latina feminine role may be embarrassments to their families.

For parents in many cultures, the love for their child may be in conflict with their internalized societal concept of lesbians and gays. Duane's parents, unable to accept their son's gayness, were reluctant to talk about his sexuality and ignored his repeated requests for books and information. Parents may chose to respond with rejection, ostracism, and/or violence, or with acceptance. Although Jeremy's mother has come to accept her son's sexual orientation, his older adult brother has isolated Jeremy from his son for the stated purpose of protecting his son from molestation by Jeremy. In contrast, Barbara's mother counseled her daughter to be happy with herself:

> We love you. We support you. And we'll defend you to the death.

Parental reactions are as varied as youths' coping strategies.

Parents may be comforted by the notion that their son or daughter's sexual orientation is just a phase or a fluke, the result of hero worship or a close friendship. Such rationalizations are common. Travis, who came out to his mother as a high school junior, was originally frustrated by his mother's unwillingness to accept what he was telling her. In his diary, he recorded, ". . . for the last five years I have known that WITHOUT QUES-TION I am gay." Later, Travis' mother began to question his feelings:

> She tells me that I've never even tried dating. . . . "You haven't even given heterosexuality a chance!" Oh, brother.

"I think that you are bisexual," rationalized another mother, "because you have a strong need for love and affection." "You need so much," she continued, "that you believe that you need it from both sexes."

A second reaction is compartmentalization by which a parent attempts to separate the person from the orientation or the orientation from sex. "It is sex, pure and simple," concluded Michael's mother, "just physical." In that one statement she has negated her son's feelings and probably alienated him.

The well-being of each lesbian and gay youth is closely related to her or his perceived or actual level of parental acceptance.

From the first two reactions comes a third, the "simple solution," and its implication that the youth is weak. "Program your mind and then the emotions and physical attractions will follow," counsels one mother. Michael's mother offers, "Don't allow yourself to get involved." This is the *Just Say No* approach. Such advice is insulting in its giver's inability to comprehend what the youth is experiencing. The inherent insensitivity leaves a youth feeling frustrated, rejected or abandoned, and angry.

Unfortunately, a parental attitude that finds excuses for feelings or behavior while not confronting them causes great difficulties for a youth who is becoming aware of her or his sexual identity. Although there is no rush to establish a sexual identity, such attitudes only result in sexual confusion and may unnecessarily delay sexual identification.

The benefits of family support

The importance of parental acceptance cannot be overstressed. An accepting family can greatly facilitate the coming-out process. Brent, age sixteen, recalls coming out to his mom:

> The words just wouldn't come out. . . . She kept guessing things and finally she got it. . . . She gave me a hug and told me she loved me. I didn't expect it to be that good.

In general, a youth's perception of family attitudes is a very important factor in overall self-esteem. The well-being of each lesbian and gay youth is closely related to her or his perceived or actual level of parental acceptance. Parental attitudes are often incorporated into a child's self-perception. Barbara came out at age twelve:

> My mother . . . said that since I was very young . . . I should wait a few months at least before deciding that this was an absolute fact. But if it turned out, indeed, that I was a lesbian, then that was fine.

"I think my mother knew," recalls a young gay man. "She wanted me to be in therapy since seven or eight, not to change me but so that I could be happy and sure of my homosexuality."

The road to a healthy self-concept

The process of coming out may involve guilt, self-hatred, self-pity, fear of nonacceptance, and denial. Successful navigation of each can lead to better understanding and self-acceptance. For those who are not successful, these feelings may impede progress. It is only the well-integrated person who can really share herself or himself with the world. In turn, clarifying oneself by self-disclosure can facilitate integration.

Coming out does not ensure success. Careful and thoughtful decisions must be made about when, to whom, and how to self-disclose, and the psychological costs must be weighed. Covert behavior and fear of disclosure can lead to psychological difficulties. The most closeted lesbian and gay adults have more personal conflict, more alienation and depression, and more negative self-esteem than their more open peers. Some lesbian and gay youths, unable to cope with deception and isolation, may run away or engage in antisocial behavior, such as prostitution.

Nonetheless, the benefits of being open usually outweigh the drawbacks. "I lost several friends," laments Heather, age seventeen, "but the real friendships I've gained are worth so much more than the superficial friendships that I've lost." "My true friends supported me and became even better friends," concludes Salim, age sixteen; "the ones who didn't accept me were truly never my friends in the first place." It has been reported that coming out may result in healthier psychological adjustment, fewer feelings of guilt and loneliness, less need for psychological counseling, more positive attitudes toward homosexuality and a positive lesbian or gay identity, and a greater fusion of sexuality and affect. One fourteen-year-old male writes:

> I was on a roller coaster where my emotions began to collide.
> Should I live, or shall I die, went through my mind when I began to hide.
> Hide from the world and hide from my mom,
> I shall rinse that away, and let my life go on.
> Thy melted snow has seeped away,
> My boots are clean, and that is good,
> I am out of the closet, just as I should!

8

Parents Should Be Supportive of Their Gay and Lesbian Children

Parents, Families, and Friends of Lesbians and Gays

Parents, Families, and Friends of Lesbians and Gays (PFLAG) is a national nonprofit organization that promotes the health and well-being of lesbian, gay, bisexual, and transgendered people, their friends, and their families.

Parents can experience a variety of first reactions when they find out their child is lesbian, gay, or bisexual. Some parents experience grief, anger, or denial. Others question why their child turned out to be gay, or they worry about their child's safety and future happiness. No matter what initial feelings arise, parents can move toward understanding, acceptance, and support. Stereotypes and misconceptions about homosexuality, as well as hatred and fear toward homosexuals, are all too common in our society. These problems can be confronted and minimized for parents and their children if families build strong support systems, seek accurate information about homosexuality, and foster open communication. Many families deepen their respect, appreciation, and enjoyment of each other through the process of learning about a child's gay, lesbian, or bisexual identity.

*W*hat do you do when you first find out that your child is gay, lesbian or bisexual?

If you're like many parents, your first reaction is "How will I ever handle this?" Most parents aren't prepared for the words, "Mom, Dad. I'm gay.". . .

We can tell you with absolute certainty that you're not alone. According to some statistics, one in every ten people in this country and around the world is gay. Therefore, approximately one in four families has an immediate family member who is gay, lesbian or bisexual, and most families have at least one gay, lesbian or bisexual member in their extended family circle.

That means that there are plenty of people out there you can talk to. We can tell you from experience that talking about it really helps. There are books to read, telephone helplines to call and people to meet who, by sharing their own experiences, can help you move forward. . . .

The second thing we can tell you is that—if you wish—you will emerge from this period with a stronger, closer relationship with your child than you have ever had before. That's been the case for all of us. But the path to that point is often not easy.

Your child's decision to be open and honest with you about something many in our society discourage took a tremendous amount of courage.

Some parents were able to take the news in stride. But many of us went through something similar to a grieving process with all the accompanying shock, denial, anger, guilt and sense of loss. So if those are the feelings with which you're dealing, they're understandable given our society's attitudes towards gays, lesbians and bisexuals.

Don't condemn yourself for the emotions you feel. But, since you love your child, you owe it to him or her—and to yourself—to move toward acceptance, understanding and support.

While it may feel as if you have lost your child, you haven't. Your child is the same person he or she was yesterday. The only thing you have lost is your own image of that child and the understanding you thought you had. That loss can be very difficult, but that image can, happily, be replaced with a new and clearer understanding of your child.

If your child is young, coming to an understanding with him or her may be crucial. Gay, lesbian and bisexual youth who are shut out by their parents have a comparatively high incidence of suicide and drug and alcohol abuse. Some teens protect themselves by putting as much distance between themselves and their parents as possible.

If your son or daughter "came out" to you voluntarily, you're probably more than halfway there already. Your child's decision to be open and honest with you about something many in our society discourage took a tremendous amount of courage. And it shows an equally tremendous amount of love, trust and commitment to their relationship with you.

Now it's up to you to match your child's courage, commitment, trust and love with your own.

Your child has not changed

Is my child different now?

We think we know and understand our children from the day they are born. We're convinced that we know what's going on inside their heads.

So when a child announces "I'm gay," and we hadn't a clue—or we knew all along but denied it to ourselves—the reactions are often shock and disorientation.

You have a dream, a vision of what your child will be, should be, can be. It's a dream that is born of your own history, of what you wanted for yourself growing up, and especially of the culture around you. Despite the fact that a significant portion of the population is gay, American society still prepares us only with heterosexual dreams for our children.

The shock and disorientation you may feel is a natural part of a type of grieving process. You have lost something: your dream for your child. You also have lost the illusion that you can read your child's mind.

Of course, when you stop to think about it, this is true for all children, straight or gay. They're always surprising us. They don't marry who we might pick for them; they don't take the job we would have chosen; they don't live where we'd like them to live. In our society, though, we're better prepared to deal with those circumstances than with our child's "non-traditional" sexual orientation.

Keep reminding yourself that your child hasn't changed. Your child is the same person that he or she was before you learned about his or her sexuality. It is your dream, your expectations, your vision that may have to change if you are to really know and understand your gay loved one.

Knowing the truth

Why did he or she have to tell us?

Some parents feel they would have been happier not knowing about their child's sexuality. They look back to before they knew and recall this time as problem-free—overlooking the distance they often felt from their child during that time.

Sometimes we try to deny what is happening—by rejecting what we're hearing ("It's just a phase; you'll get over it"); by shutting down ("if you choose that lifestyle, I don't want to hear about it"); or by not registering the impact of what we're being told ("That's nice, dear, and what do you want for dinner?"). These are all natural reactions.

It is important to accept and understand your child's sexuality because homosexuality and bisexuality are not a phase.

However, if you did not know the truth about your child's sexuality, you would never really know your child. A large part of his or her life would be kept secret from you, and you would never really know the whole person.

It is important to accept and understand your child's sexuality because homosexuality and bisexuality are not a phase.

While people may experiment for some time with their sexuality, someone who has reached the point of telling a parent that he or she is gay is not usually going through a phase. Generally, he or she has given long and hard thought to understanding and acknowledging his or her sexual orientation.

So if you're wondering, "Is she sure?" the answer will almost always be "yes." Telling a parent that you think you're gay involves overcoming too many negative stereotypes and taking far too much risk for anyone to take that step lightly or prematurely.

The fact that your son or daughter told you is a sign of his or her love and need for your support and understanding. It took a lot of courage. And it shows a very strong desire for an open, honest relationship with you—a relationship in which you can love your child for who he or she is, rather than for who you want him or her to be.

Love and trust

Why didn't our child tell us before?

One difficult realization for you may be the recognition that your child has probably been thinking this through for months, even years, and is only now telling you. It's easy to misinterpret this as a lack of trust, lack of love, or a reflection on your parenting. And it's painful to realize that you don't know your child as well as you thought you did, and that you have been excluded from a part of his or her life.

To some extent, this is true in all parenting relationships whether the child is gay or straight. There's a necessary separation between parent and child as the child moves toward adulthood. Your child may reach conclusions you would not have reached, and will do it without consulting you.

But, in this case, it is particularly hard because the conclusion your child has reached is so important and, in many cases, so unexpected. You may have been shut out of your child's thinking for a long period of time.

Gay people may hold back from their parents as long as possible because it has taken them a long time to figure out what they're feeling themselves. In other words, gay, lesbian and bisexual youth often recognize at an early age that they feel "different," but it may take years before they can put a name to these feelings.

Because we still live in a society that misunderstands or is fearful of gay people, it takes time for them to acknowledge their sexuality to themselves. Gay people have often internalized self-hate or insecurity about their sexual identity. It may take time for someone to think through and work up the courage to tell a parent. Even if you feel your child should have known they could tell you anything, remember that our culture's treatment of homosexuality says "don't ask, don't tell."

So, even as you may grieve for not having been able to help your child through that period—or even if you believe that the outcome would have been different if you had been involved earlier—understand that your child probably could not have told you any sooner. Most importantly, doing so now is an invitation to a more open and honest relationship.

Why people are gay

Why is my child gay?

Parents often ask this question for a number of reasons: they may be grieving over losing an image of their child; they feel they did something wrong; they feel that someone "led" their child into homosexuality; or they wonder if there is a biological cause of homosexuality.

Some parents react with shock, denial and anger to the news that their child is gay. One response is to wonder, "How could she do this to me?" This is not a rational reaction, but it is a human response to pain.

We liken this reaction to a grieving process: here, you are grieving over losing an image of your child. As you work through your feelings, you may discover that the only thing your child has "done" to you is to trust that your relationship could grow as a result of you knowing the truth about him or her.

You may feel that your child has been led into homosexuality by someone else. It is a popular misconception that homosexuals "recruit." The truth is that no one "made" your child gay. He or she has most likely known that he or she was "different" for a very long time—no person or group of people "converted" your child.

Other parents feel that their parenting is the cause of their child's sexual identity. For years, psychology and psychiatry have bandied around theories that homosexuality is caused by parental personality types—the dominant female, the weak male—or by the absence of same-gender role models. Those theories are no longer accepted within psychiatry and psychology, and part of PFLAG's work focuses on erasing these myths and misconceptions from our popular culture.

Gay people have often internalized self-hate or insecurity about their sexual identity.

Gay people come from all types of families. Some have dominant mothers, while others may have dominant fathers. Gay men, lesbians and bisexuals are only children and they're youngest, middle and oldest children. They come from families with siblings who are gay and families with siblings who are not gay. Many come from what society would consider "model" families.

Many parents wonder if there is a genetic or biological basis to homosexuality. While there are some studies on homosexuality and genetics, there are no conclusive studies to date on the "cause" of homosexuality. In the absence of this data, we would encourage you to ask yourself why it is important for you to know why.

Does support or love for your child rely on your ability to point to a cause? Do we ask heterosexual people to justify their sexuality that way? Remember that gay, lesbian and bisexual people exist in every walk of life, religion, nationality and racial background. Therefore, all gay people, like straight people, are very different and have come into their sexual identity in very different ways. Although we may be curious, it is really not that important to know why your child is gay in order to support and love him or her.

Discomfort with homosexuality

Why am I uncomfortable with his or her sexuality?
The apprehension you may feel is a product of our culture. Homophobia is too pervasive in our society to be banished easily from our consciousness. As long as homophobia exists, any gay person and any parent of a gay, lesbian or bisexual youth has some very real and legitimate fears and concerns.

Many parents may confront another source of guilt. Parents who see

themselves as "liberal," who believe they have put sexual prejudice behind them—even those who have gay friends—are sometimes stunned to
recognize that they are uncomfortable when it is their kid who is gay.
These parents not only have to grapple with deep-rooted fears of homosexuality, but also have the added burden of thinking they shouldn't feel
the way they do. It helps to concentrate on real concerns: what your child
needs most from you now. Try not to focus on the guilt. It is baseless, and
it accomplishes nothing for yourself or for your child.

Getting help

Should we consult a psychiatrist or psychologist?

Consulting a therapist in the hopes of changing your child's sexual
orientation is pointless. Homosexuality is not a disease to be "cured." Homosexuality is a natural way of being.

Because homosexuality is not "chosen," you cannot "change your
child's mind." The American Psychological Association and the American
Medical Association have taken the official position that it would be un-
ethical to even try to change the sexual orientation of a gay person. In
1997, the American Psychological Association again publically cautioned
against so-called "reparative therapy," also known as conversion therapy.

But there are situations where it can be helpful to consult people experienced with family issues and sexual orientation. You may want to talk
to someone about your own feelings and how to work through them. You
may feel that you and your child need help communicating clearly
through this period. Or you may recognize that your child is unhappy
and needs help with self-acceptance.

Gay people come from all types of families.

Once again, gay people often have trouble accepting themselves and
their sexual identity. In this circumstance, self-rejection could be a dangerous emotional state. . . .

There are a variety of resources for help, information and advice. We
encourage you to explore your options and to use those best suited for
you and your family. . . .

Attitudes are changing

*Will my child be ostracized, have trouble finding or keeping a job, or even be
physically attacked?*

All of these things are possible. It depends on where your son or
daughter lives what kind of job he or she takes—but attitudes toward homosexuality have begun to change, and are now changing relatively
quickly. There are many places where your child can live and work relatively free of discrimination.

Unfortunately, societal change is often slow—just look at how long it
took for women to achieve voting rights in this country.

Progress is often also accompanied by backlash. Until more individuals and more organizations become advocates for gay rights, until homophobia is eradicated in our society, your child does face some significant challenges.

Religion

How do I reconcile this with my religion?

For some parents, this may be the most difficult issue to face. For others, it's a non-issue.

It is true that some religions continue to condemn homosexuality. But even within these religions, there are respected leaders who believe that their church's position of condemnation is unconscionable.

In 1997, the U.S. Catholic bishops issued a pastoral statement urging parents to love and support their gay children. In a 1994 pastoral letter, the U.S. Episcopal bishops wrote, "As it can be for heterosexual persons, the experience of steadfast love can be for homosexual persons an experience of God."

There are many places where your child can live and work relatively free of discrimination.

Many mainstream American religions have now taken official stands in support of gay rights. Some have gone further. The Methodist Church, for example, has developed a network of reconciling congregations welcoming gays, lesbians and bisexuals. Since 1991, the United Church of Christ has had a denominational policy stating that sexual orientation should not be a barrier to ordination. In the Episcopal Church, the denomination's legislative body has declared that gay people have a full and equal claim with all other people upon the church.

You will still hear people quote the Bible in defense of their prejudice against gay people. But many Biblical scholars dispute any anti-gay interpretations of Biblical texts. . . .

Telling others

How do we tell family and friends?

Just as "coming out" is difficult for gay people, the coming-out process is equally difficult for parents. Many, upon learning their child is gay, go right into the closet. As they struggle with accepting their child's sexual orientation, they often worry about other people finding out. There is the challenge of fielding such questions as, "Has he got a girlfriend?" and "So when is she going to get married?"

Many of us found that our fears were far worse than reality. Some of us held off for years in telling our own parents—our children's grandparents—only to have them respond, "We knew that quite a while ago."

Our advice to you is the same advice we give to gay, lesbian and bisexual individuals. Learn more about the changing attitudes within medical, psychiatric, religious, professional and political circles. There are plenty of "authorities" you can quote as allies in defense of equal rights for gay people. . . .

Practice what you would say just like you might practice for a public speaking engagement, for a job interview, for boosting your assertivness, or for anything new to you that makes you afraid or nervous.

One parent says, "I used to go in the bathroom and close the door and practice saying to the mirror, 'I have a lesbian daughter' and saying it with pride. And it helped. But you really do have to practice.". . .

You may get some negative or, at the least, insensitive comments from relatives, friends or co-workers. But you'll probably find that those comments are fewer than you now fear.

Remember that your child has been down this road already. He or she may even be able to help.

And remember also that who you tell about your child's sexuality should be a decision that both of you discuss and reach together. . . .

Support

How can I support my child?

As a parent, you have to take care of yourself and your child. PFLAG is here to help you with your individual needs so that you can be an even better parent.

Reading [information like this viewpoint] is the first step to supporting your child—you have shown that you are open to new information and hopefully you are now better informed.

Supporting your child now should be a natural extension of your general support as a parent: we need to talk, listen and learn together.

Every child needs different things from his or her parents. It is up to you to learn how to communicate with him or her about their needs and issues surrounding sexuality.

There are plenty of "authorities" you can quote as allies in defense of equal rights for gay people.

Some parents find that they are better able to understand and support their child by recognizing the similarities and differences in their own life experiences. In some cases it may help to talk about how you have dealt with hurtful incidents.

But in other cases you must recognize that discrimination based on sexual orientation is hurtful in a unique way.

Here, you can support your child by educating yourself as thoroughly as possible about homosexuality and by helping to bring it out of hiding in our society. It's the hiding that allows the prejudice and discrimination to survive.

The future

Will I ever learn to deal with this new knowledge?

A psychiatrist answered the question this way: "Once most people adjust to the reality of their child's sexual orientation, they feel like they've had a whole new world opened to them.

"First, they become acquainted with a side of their child they never knew. They now are included in their child's life. Usually, they get closer. And the parents begin to meet the gay community and understand that these are people just like any other community."

"Once most people adjust to the reality of their child's sexual orientation, they feel like they've had a whole new world opened to them."

Another way to answer this question is to let some parents speak for themselves:

> "I hit a point where I was feeling sad and thinking what would I say when people asked, 'How is Gary?' And then it occurred to me: Gary's fine. I'm the one who's not. And once I reached that point, it was easier . . . as we met Gary's friends, we found them to be wonderful people and realized that he's really part of a pretty terrific community. So what's the problem? It's society's problem. That's when we figured we were over the hump."
>
> —Mother of a gay son

> "I'd say that reading and learning more about sexual orientation is what helped me most . . . laying to rest some of the myths I had heard. . . . So the more I learned, the angrier I got, and the more I wanted to change society instead of my son."
>
> —Mother of a gay son

> "I think the turning point for me was when I read more about it, and read that most kids who can accept their sexuality say they feel calmer, happier and more confident. And of course, that's what I wanted for my child and I sure didn't want to be what was standing in the way of that."
>
> —Father of a gay son

> "I was teary-eyed for three months off and on. But we've always had a very good relationship. It has never changed from that. We never had an instant's question of our love for him, and we both assured him immediately that we loved him. And since then, our relationship with our son is strengthened, because we have a bond simply because we know what he is up against in our society."
>
> —Mother of a gay son

> "It's really important to talk about it, to know that you're not alone, that there are other people who have had this experience and are dealing with it in a positive way. And the benefit is that you establish a good relationship with your

child. Parents want to parent. They don't, generally speaking, want to be isolated from their kid."

—Mother of a lesbian daughter

"For me, it was my son's saying to me, 'Dad, I'm the same person I was before.' Now it's been six months, and I realize even more that really, nothing has changed in his life. It was our perception of him, I guess."

—Father of a gay son

"I have to tell you, there are so many pluses now. You begin to recognize what an incredible child you have to share this with you and to want you to be a part of their lives. . . . [Look at] the trust that has been placed in your hands and how much guts it took to do that."

—Father of a lesbian daughter

9

Parents Should Encourage Their Gay and Lesbian Children to Become Heterosexual

Mark Hartzell

Mark Hartzell is director of Harvest USA Mid-South and an ordained teaching elder in the Presbyterian Church in America. Harvest USA is a Christian organization that focuses on helping people who want to be free of the influences of pornography and homosexuality.

When teenagers tell their Christian parents they are gay, common parental reactions vary from devastation to repulsion. Several principles can guide parents to help themselves and their children heal from such a fall from grace. Parents need to carefully discern the situation and take it seriously, but not feel hopeless or overwhelmed by it. By admitting their own need for spiritual healing, parents can lead a son or daughter in repentance by example. Truth telling and gentle instruction in the Gospel is essential to healing families. Conflict can be expected, and only by setting reasonable boundaries can parents bring children into healthy, life-affirming relationships. Finally, parents must develop a strong support system and ultimately allow God to direct a child's healing process.

You've stumbled upon disturbing news. Perhaps your 16-year-old daughter has been attending the local "gay-straight" alliance in her school and has come home with the bombshell that she is a lesbian. Or you have discovered your 15-year-old son's correspondence on the Internet with another male—and it's obvious they have very intimate knowledge of each other. Or maybe your son has just expressed some questions to you that make you wonder 'whether he is gay.' Or you've found homosexual pornography in his room. Or your daughter has been reading some pro-gay literature and passing it on to you.

The grief cycle has hit you—like an express train broadsiding you. But it is not from your 25-year-old son or daughter, living with a lover in a faraway city—but right in your own home, under your nose night and day. You feel repulsed, betrayed, helpless, isolated, resentful, and perhaps devastated by waves of shame and self-pity. How should you respond as a Christian parent? And is there hope?

Carefully discern the situation

"Do not answer a fool according to his folly, or you will be like him yourself. Answer a fool according to his folly, or he will be wise in his own eyes." (Proverbs 26:4–5)

Learn to discern. Is he just trying to be outrageous and shocking by appearing to embrace the outlandish—or something more? Homosexuality is touted as something exotic and chic—like that wide haircut or those unusual body piercings. Is she simply trying on the latest fashion, to see how it fits—or enmeshed in something deeper? The exotic can easily become the erotic, and every act of rebellion also has elements of unbelief woven in, so take matters seriously—but avoid making mountains out of molehills by overreacting.

Lead your daughter or son in repentance. Ask Christ for the grace to admit your shortcomings, yes, your failures as a parent.

It is appropriate to grieve the effects of the Fall, and you can expect to feel all the stages of the grief cycle (shock, denial, anger, fear, numbness . . .). But hysteria on your part is not going to build the bridges you need to build. Ask Christ to make you more "shockproof" as a parent of a teenager. But also more sensitive to the desperate cries and throbbing aches of the heart of your teen for intimacy, belonging, and adventure. Adolescence is a tough time for most teens, and as they come to terms with who they are as a man or woman they need the wisdom of those who have gone before them.

Personally repent

"When I kept silent, my bones wasted away . . . then I acknowledged my sin to you and did not cover up my iniquity. I said, 'I will confess my transgressions to the Lord—and you forgave the guilt of my sin.'" (Psalm 32:3,5)

Being honest with yourself means you must be willing to admit your own daily need of the Gospel. Where are the areas of pride, fear, and unbelief that you need to honestly repent of as a parent? Lead your daughter or son in repentance. Ask Christ for the grace to admit your shortcomings, yes, your failures as a parent. Fact is, none of us had perfect parents—and none of us will be perfect parents. Life in a fallen world means that there is indeed something wrong with everything—so that even our most intimate relationships don't work out like they should.

Patterns of emotional distancing between a child and the same-sex parent happen early in life, long before anyone is aware of what is really going on. And patterns of manipulation and overcontrol by the opposite-sex parent are likewise subtle and not immediately apparent to anyone involved. Your teen may not be aware of what has happened and probably won't be able to verbalize "what went wrong," but don't be daunted by this. In fact, if she has already bought completely into the "just born this way" myth, then your attempts to talk about your family dynamics may well be met with hostility and/or denial. She has a lot invested in such "no fault" thinking that wants to make sure you feel OK as a parent. She may not allow you to "be a sinner" in front of her—or others.

"I'm OK, you're OK," is a common element of gay ideology—and indeed all pop culture today. But you must continue to invite her to the truth, and the doorway to her realizing her sin often will be your own humility and open repenting before her.

Gently instruct your children

"Those who oppose him he must gently instruct, in the hope that God will grant them repentance leading them to a knowledge of the truth, and that they will come to their senses and escape from the trap of the devil, who has taken them captive to do his will." (2 Timothy 2:25)

Most often, there is an earnest plea for attention going on. And usually this isn't the first time that your teen has "cried out" for attention. But whenever the emotional and relational needs for same-sex affection, affirmation and identification are not met early on in life, then it is common for those emotional desires to become sexualized during adolescence. When the cup of life is jostled by the buffets of adolescent hormones, it is the substance of what has been filling that cup for many years that spills out. And decisions that are then made on the basis of those heart-level needs can either lead to redemptive deliverance or further enslavement and bondage to sin.

Even if the past seems a total disaster, there is hope through the power of the risen Christ for relationships to be different now and in the future. Your teen needs parents willing to take the risks of bold love and uncompromising instruction in the path of life. He needs a father, a male figure who is strong and courageous in speaking the truth in love—a dad who is willing to shatter the silence even on admittedly uncomfortable subjects. He needs a mother who is open-handed before the Lord, not demanding of perfection or overprotective and manipulative but willing to love with the truth.

Truth-telling in the home must become the standard—for everyone. No "white lies" are allowed; all deception, even that which seems innocent, must be ruthlessly weeded out. Your teen needs to be pursued with the truth and not allowed to wander in the wasteland of post-modern ethics where "it can't be wrong when it feels so right."

Set reasonable boundaries

"But as for me and my household, we will serve the Lord." (Joshua 24:15)

If your young person is under age 18 and/or still living under your roof and authority, there need to be reasonable guidelines agreed upon by all.

Life with any number of sinners under one roof means that sparks will fly.

Conflict will happen, so expect it. And sexual sin—of any type—should not be winked at. Certainly pornography of any kind should not be tolerated, for all sexual sin begins with impurity in the mind and lust in the heart. All inappropriate, destructive intimacy (with the same or opposite sex) must be 'put off' ever as healthy, genuine intimacy is "put on."

Watch for emotional dependencies just as much as sexual activity, for the one can quickly lead to the other. You cannot allow manipulation—or threats—from your teen. The consequences must be made clear to all concerned. While every annoyance cannot be the cause for discipline, redemptive parental discipline must be brought to bear for transgressions involving disobedience, dishonesty, or disrespect. When boundaries are willfully crossed, such rebellion must not be minimized or avoided but rather dealt with straightforwardly.

Healthy discipline involves natural consequences that are meaningful and respectful to your teen and that are carried out in a timely way. Above all, you want to ask Christ not to let you exasperate your teen (Ephesians 6:4) even as you must give him or her significant, life-giving boundaries.

Go for the heart

"Watch over your heart with all diligence, for from it flow the springs of life." (Proverbs 4:23)

Don't be fooled—homosexuality is not just about sex. "Being gay" is a gospel issue, a heart issue reflecting the core of our being. Such heart cravings cannot be dealt with by behavior modification techniques. Avoid "just say no" moralism. More rules is not the answer—changing your relationship with your teen is closer to the target. You will want to "just fix this," but it is not your job to fix your teen—and you can't fix the heart of another person even if you wanted to.

God alone is Lord of the heart, and He alone can change a sinner—any sinner—from the inside out. The root issues that give rise to homosexual longings—such as pride, fear, unbelief, anger, rebellion, rejection, envy—are the core issues that require ongoing repentance from us all. But change doesn't usually happen overnight, and never in a vacuum. The idols of our hearts are not easily or willingly replaced without a battle.

Set the pace in pursuing change yourself, at the heart level, and then you will be able to invite your teen to pursue deep change ALONG WITH you. Your teen needs to know Christ better, and so do you.

Enlist support

"Bear one another's burdens, and thus fulfill the law of Christ." (Galatians 6:2)

Because change doesn't happen in a vacuum—for you OR your teen—you need other spiritual support in this battle. You need a friend or two with whom you can be completely frank and honest about your own heart aches and issues, your own griefs and disappointments—someone who will love you enough to walk beside you along this often painful path of change.

You cannot handle this alone—and Jesus designed life that way. It is not an admission of weakness to own your need of the prayers of other believers, but an admission that the Body of Christ really is what God intends for it to be. You must risk opening up your heart because you need the specific prayers of other Christians to not only survive but to thrive.

Find a pastor, an elder, a counselor, a friend, or a support group such as those at Harvest USA.

Facing the wreckage of life as a parent in a fallen world can be tiring, frustrating, overwhelming. But you don't need to face it alone. Christ knows all about your pain—and that of your teenager. He tasted and drank the cup of agony and wrath—He has been there and done that. And because homosexuality or using the label "gay" is an "identity" issue, it is just the sort of problem that Jesus specializes in. He continually offers us a new identity, so that we are no longer defined by our pain, our sin, or our failures.

The Cross shows us a Savior who, though sinless, became sin for us—that we might be clothed in His righteousness in the great exchange (2 Corinthians 5:21). And His resurrection proves that all He promised is true. Christ's victory over death means that there is hope for you—and your son or daughter. He longs that we might have life, and have it to the full (John 10:10). Not an easy, pain-free life, but a life of surprising beauty, of ravishing intimacy, and abundant adventure nonetheless. For He is with us, and He is Life itself.

10

Canada Leads North America in Gay Marriage Rights

DeNeen L. Brown

DeNeen L. Brown is a reporter for the Washington Post.

In June 2003 Canada legalized same-sex marriage throughout the nation. Gays and lesbians around the world praised the decision as a milestone in global human rights. However, strong opposition has been expressed from several organizations in Canada and the United States that want to limit marriage exclusively to heterosexual couples. In the wake of the Canadian decision, same-sex couples from around the world have traveled to Canada to be married. Many believe that Canada has become the foremost proponent of gay marriage in North America.

The betrothed wore black suits and held hands as they marched down the hall of the courthouse in Toronto [Canada]. "The Michaels" nervously stood before a judge and repeated these vows:

"I, Michael, take you, Michael, to be my lawful wedded spouse, to have and to hold from this day forward in whatever circumstance or experience life may hold for us."

After the vows, the judge declared: "I, by the virtue of the powers invested in me by the marriage act, do hereby declare you, Michael and Michael, publicly and affectionately known as the Michaels, to be lawful wedded spouses."

And with that the crowd gathered for them at the Ontario Superior Court applauded. Cameras flashed, and the men, Michael Leshner, 55, and Michael Stark, 45, kissed.

A landmark in gay marriage

The day [June 21, 2003] was a dramatic culmination, they said, for the gay rights movement in North America as Canada became the first country on this continent to grant the right of legal, government-sanctioned marriage to gay and lesbian couples.[1]

"Today is Day One for millions of gays and lesbians in Canada and around the world," Leshner said after the ceremony. "This is a wonderful, wonderful human rights story and a wonderful love story. . . . This judgment puts a stake in the heart of homophobia."

Hundreds of gay and lesbian couples have wed in Ontario since an appeals court issued a historic decision [in June 2003] that changed the definition of marriage in the province from the union of a man and woman to the union of two people. Prime Minister Jean Chretien has announced that his government would draft legislation legalizing same-sex marriages in all of Canada.

The Ontario court's ruling declared "the dignity of persons in same-sex relationships is violated by the exclusion of same-sex couples from the institution of marriage." The ruling took effect immediately.

Gay and lesbian American couples travel to Canada

Court officials in Ontario report that dozens of American same-sex couples have crossed the border to register and exchange vows, hoping that some day their Canadian licenses will be recognized back home. Tour companies have created packages aimed at attracting same-sex couples in the United States to travel to Canada for weddings. Toronto's City Hall [planned] to remain open for [Gay] Pride weekend, June 28–29, to give couples a chance to marry.

"I'm hoping more Americans come up here and get married and erode the Defense of Marriage Act," said Kyle Rae, a Toronto city councilor. "I think as more and more Americans come up to get married, states will have a difficult time not recognizing a sovereign state's marriage license."

> *"The dignity of persons in same-sex relationships is violated by the exclusion of same-sex couples from the institution of marriage."*

[Only Massachusetts] recognizes same-sex marriages. Vermont recognizes civil unions, which give gay and lesbian couples the benefits and responsibilities of marriage but are separate from a legal marriage. The U.S. Congress passed the Defense of Marriage Act in 1996, which defines marriage as a legal union between a man and a woman as husband and wife.

Canada does not require residency for marriage, and marriage licenses issued in Canada have been accepted in the United States. Gay and lesbian rights advocates in the United States are hoping Canada's move to legalize same-sex marriage will encourage court challenges to marriage laws in the United States.

Gary Buseck, executive director of Gay and Lesbian Advocates and Defenders, based in Boston, said he hoped that since Canada was "our

---

1. The Canadian government was given until July 12, 2004, to align gay marriage law with the Canadian Charter of Rights and Freedoms. Ontario, British Columbia, and Quebec appealed the mandate and lost.

closest neighbor, sharing many of our values" the case would "speak strongly to American courts seeing that another society can make this step and the sky doesn't fall in."

The decision to allow same-sex marriages is the latest in a string of bold stands in Canada, some of which have upset U.S. officials. Over the objections of some U.S. officials, Canada announced it would decriminalize possession of small amounts of marijuana. Despite heavy pressure from the United States, Canada refused to join the U.S.-led invasion of Iraq [in spring 2003].

A strong current of anti-Americanism has long simmered just below the surface of Canadian politics. But U.S.-Canadian relations, some reported, reached a historic low earlier this year [2003] when a Liberal Party member of Parliament called Americans "bastards" and Chretien's spokeswoman resigned after reportedly calling Bush a "moron" because of his policy on Iraq.

Another move toward equality

On June 10 [2003] the Ontario Court of Appeals declared that any law prohibiting same-sex couples from marrying violated Canada's Charter of Rights. Discrimination based on sexual orientation has been prohibited in Canada since 1995. The court rejected the attorney general's argument that marriage should be exclusively a heterosexual institution.

The court argued that "the encouragement of procreation and child-rearing" should not exclude same-sex couples from marriage, pointing out that same-sex couples in Canada are allowed to have children through adoption, surrogate pregnancy or donor insemination. "Importantly, procreation and child-rearing are not the only purposes of marriage, or the only reason why couples choose to marry," the court said. . . .

> *The proposed legislation recognizing homosexual marriages would make it clear that religious groups would not be required to perform same-sex weddings.*

The federal government chose not to appeal the Ontario court decision. "There is evolution in society and according to the interpretation of the courts, they concluded these unions should be legal in Canada," Chretien said.

Chretien said the proposed legislation recognizing homosexual marriages would make it clear that religious groups would not be required to perform same-sex weddings. The federal government's proposal will be made public within weeks. Until it is approved by the Canadian House of Commons, gay and lesbian couples will be able to marry only in the province of Ontario.

Chretien's proposal prompted immediate criticism. In the province of Alberta, Premier Ralph Klein threatened to block the federal government's attempt to impose same-sex marriages in Alberta. Klein said Alberta would use a "notwithstanding clause," a Canadian constitutional provision that allows provinces to withdraw from federal decisions.

"The Alberta government believes that marriage is fundamentally a union between a man and a woman," said the provincial justice minister, Dave Hancock. "Alberta law will continue to recognize this."

In the United States, some groups have readied for a national battle against gay marriage. In May [2003] several members of Congress introduced the Federal Marriage Amendment, which defines marriage as a union between one man and one woman without exceptions.

"The recent court action in Ontario, Canada, illustrates the very reason I introduced the Federal Marriage Amendment," Rep. Marilyn Musgrave (R-Colo.) said in a statement. "For over 200 years in the United States, marriage has been known as a union between a woman and a man. . . . My bill ensures the question of homosexual marriage is stricken from unelected judges and placed in the hands of the American people and their elected representatives."

The meaning of marriage to same-sex couples

Within hours after the Ontario court decision, couples rushed to wed.

"We didn't want to wait another nanosecond," Leshner said. "We had been living together 22 years. How long would two straight people in love wait?"

Joyce Barnett, 50, married Alison Kemper, 47, . . . at City Hall. "We moved so quickly because we didn't want to be caught holding a license," Barnett said. "We picked up the license on Tuesday, the day the decision came down." Barnett said the ceremony was short.

Barnett said that getting the right to marry made her feel like a complete person. "I know there are all kinds of people, both gay and straight, who don't choose to marry," she said. "But to be denied the choice really sends the message you are not quite as good as anyone else."

Rae, the Toronto city councilor, wed his longtime partner, Mark Reid, during a ceremony . . . behind a rainbow of balloons at a downtown art gallery. There were no wedding rings, no vows were exchanged, no rice was thrown and no champagne was drunk.

"A wedding is determined by the mothers-in-law. And we are established, older men. We want simplicity," said Rae, who wore black trousers, a black jacket and a dark shirt and tie.

Rae and Reid say they have been together nine years, but Rae said they never previously thought of marrying.

"For most of my activist life, marriage was seen as a ritual or relationship that had been denied to us. It was constructed as heterosexual and denied to my community," he said. "As the straight community held onto it, it became, 'Why would you want to? If they feel so threatened by it?' Now, my feeling is we have an opportunity to redefine marriage."

11

Gay Marriage in Canada Is a Form of Religious Persecution

Deborah Gyapong

Deborah Gyapong currently writes for several Canadian Christian publications and Web sites, including ChristianWeek *and* Christianity.ca, *and formerly served as a senior producer for the Canadian Broadcasting Corporation (CBC).*

Several Canadian Christian and Muslim leaders view the nation's gay marriage law as part of a growing trend of religious persecution. They believe that religious people are being forced to accept gay marriage when it goes against their beliefs about the primacy of the traditional family. Moreover, liberal lawmakers are attempting to silence religious opposition to homosexuality by labeling dissenters as extremists. Similarly, by including homosexuals as an identifiable group in the hate crimes sections of the criminal code, they are trying to remove freedom of speech by classifying resistance to gay marriage as a crime.

"Persecution is not coming to Canada. It's already here," says William Oosterman, pastor of Ottawa's Westboro Baptist Church. He was one of about a dozen speakers who addressed thousands of Canadians who marched to Parliament Hill from the Supreme Court of Canada August 22 [2003] to show their support for the traditional definition of marriage.[1]

Oosterman warned that no matter what Prime Minister Jean Chrétien promises in regards to protection for religious faith communities that do not support same-sex marriage, the *Charter of Rights and Freedoms* offers no protection. "Do not believe their deception," he says.

He laid out a litany of court cases where Christians have been overruled or fined for acting according to their beliefs—from Scott Brockie, the Christian printer who refused to do work for a gay and lesbian group,

---

1. The Canadian government was given until July 12, 2004, to align gay marriage with the Canadian Charter of Rights and Freedoms. Ontario, British Columbia, and Quebec appealed the mandate and lost.

to Hugh Owen, who put an ad in a Saskatoon paper listing Bible references opposing homosexual behaviour, to the attacks of the [British Columbia] College of Teachers against Christian teacher Chris Kempling for writing letters to the editor outlining his views on homosexuality.

In each case, Oosterman asked, "Where was the Charter?" in defending their freedom of speech and of religion.

"Real power in Canada is not in the legislature or in the prime minister's office. It's down the street, behind closed doors, in the hands of unelected judges," he says. "Democracy is dying.

"Paul Martin [Prime Minister Chrétien's successor], you are too late! The prime minister is a body hiding behind the skirts of the judges of Canada and Ontario."

Gay marriage and hate crimes legislation

Derek Rogusky, senior researcher with Focus on the Family Canada, sounded a similar alarm. He told the rally that [member of Parliament (MP)] Svend Robinson's Bill C-250, which would include "sexual orientation" as an identifiable group in the hate crimes sections of the Criminal Code, will be voted on September 22 [2003] a mere two days after MPs return to the House of Commons.

That bill, he says, would potentially stop any criticism against same-sex marriage or homosexual activity and "even make parts of the Bible illegal."

He said it's clear from the research that traditional marriage is good not only for men and women and their children, but for society as a whole.

"There is a lower dependency on health and welfare services and lower crime rates when families flourish," he says.

"Be prepared for the Liberal hate campaign."

Members of Parliament have been told they can "vote with their conscience" when the matter comes before them . . . , but some say that doesn't mean much.

"A promise of a free vote in Parliament is meaningless if the courts have already made the law," says Cheryl Gallant, a Canadian Alliance MP from the Ottawa Valley riding of Renfrew-Nippissing-Pembroke.

She warns that same-sex marriage is the perfect wedge issue for the Liberals to continue their divide and conquer strategy to remain in power through patronage. "Be prepared for the Liberal hate campaign," she says, warning that those who oppose same-sex marriage will be painted as extremists.

Lorraine McNamara of REAL [Realistic, Equal, Active, for Life] Women of Canada pointed out that homosexual legal activity to push for change through the Charter is financed by taxpayers' dollars, but those opposed to their agenda have to raise their own funding. And, she says no other countries have allowed the courts to make such a drastic change in the definition of marriage.

State interference

Justice Minister Martin Cauchon, "scoffs that religion is interfering with the state," [McNamara] says. "The state is interfering with religion.

"The bedrock of this society is stable family units of a mother and father and children. The government should be encouraging it," she adds. . . .

Imam Gamal Solaiman of Ottawa's Muslim community spoke of "the infallible words of God" and thousands of years of marriage as a union of a man and a woman. "We believe this is the natural, respectful and truthful way. Any other way is dangerous for our future and for future generations."

Christians attending the rally agreed. "We wish to see Canada morally renewed," says Peter Au, who spoke for the thousands from Chinese churches in Toronto and Montreal who attended the rally. "We constitute a significant part of the Canadian demographic.

"We respect individuals who have different lifestyles and different belief systems. Our respect springs from love. But God's love does not compromise His holiness. Let the silent majority speak out loud and clear."

12

Christians Should Support Gay Marriage in Canada

Vaughn Roste

Vaughn Roste is a Canadian freelance writer and musician who holds degrees in theology and music from two Christian church institutions.

Many incorrectly assume that all religious people oppose same-sex marriage. On the contrary, a faithful religious contingent strongly supports gay marriage in Canada. Canadian Christians should become leaders in the gay marriage movement because it will help the church increase its relevancy to contemporary society. Some of the many reasons for Christians to support gay marriage include their commitment to equal rights, freedom of religion, and the compassionate teachings of Jesus; their understanding that marriage has evolved into a modern institution; and their support for the separation of church and state.

Having attended several debates about same-sex marriage thus far, it is still my firm conviction that there has yet to be proposed a single reason why same-sex marriage is bad for the country that is not based on religion or that has not been sufficiently countered. Most of the reasons proposed against same-sex marriage are in fact arguments against homosexuality in general, which is a useless argument to be had in the first place (as if one chooses between homo- or heterosexuality based on logic). While I can understand the opposition on religious grounds, I cannot understand why those same people cannot appreciate that other religious people might legitimately disagree with them. It seems shocking to some that Christians could support same-sex marriage, yet there has been a faithful contingent of religious pro-same-sex marriage supporters at every rally or event (for or against) that I have attended thus far. I thought it may be timely to explain how some Christians can do this—and further, why all Christians should. Opposition to same-sex marriage need not be labelled religious, as the Christian camp is by no means united on this matter. Naturally, I can only speak from the perspective of my own religion, Christianity, but I thought I would offer my own contribution to the debate: ten reasons why Christians should support same-sex marriage.

Ten reasons to support same-sex marriage

1. *Because Christians support equal rights for all Canadians (indeed, all humans).* The "special rights" argument is patently false—this is obviously a clear case of all citizens being treated exactly equally with respect to all of the societal approbations that are associated with marriage: inheritance, taxation, hospital visitation rights etc. What is special about gays and lesbians being granted the same rights as heterosexual couples already have?

2. *Because Christians have long benefited from the freedom of religion in this country, and would want to continue to respect that in the future.* Even if you personally don't approve of same-sex marriage, you might at least recognize that there are several other denominations who are in favour of same-sex marriage: the Society of Friends, Metropolitan Community Church, Lambda Christian Church, and the United Church of Canada are only four Edmonton examples. To deny any religious groups' belief to practice same-sex marriage in Canada violates a belief in the freedom of religion for all.

3. *Because modern Christians realize that marriage has nothing to do with procreation.* Often a primary objection to same-sex marriages is that they cannot bear children. Not only is this narrow-minded and untrue (many creative solutions are available to the same-sex couple that desires to raise children), it's a double-standard. No one tests heterosexuals for their fertility or desire to raise children before determining their suitability for marriage—on the contrary, churches today regularly marry couples known to be infertile (post-menopausal women being only one example). Inasmuch as any heterosexual couple that has remained childless has been recognized as married by the church, it is hypocritical to resort to this fallacious logic in the same-sex marriage debate.

Same-sex marriage can be seen as enhancing and strengthening marriage instead of the opposite.

---

4. *Because Christians should support marriage in all of its forms.* Some claim that same-sex marriage is an attack on family values, but this is incorrect. On the contrary, it is an attempt by GLBT [gay, lesbian, bisexual, transgendered] people to be legally recognized as having families in the first place. It is a non sequitur to claim that only the "traditional" nuclear family model is legitimate when less than half of Canadian families conform to this model currently anyways. Same-sex marriage can be seen as enhancing and strengthening marriage instead of the opposite.

5. *Because Christians realize that the Church has been discriminatory in the past and would seek amends for that.* Formerly the Church denigrated "homosexual promiscuity" without making available any other option (a recognized covenanted relationship). The Christian support of same-sex marriage thus can end a hypocritical po-

sition of the Church and give the Church more relevance to contemporary society. Many agree that Christians should be opposed to discrimination in any form. The "have-your-relationships-but-don't-call-it-marriage" argument is specious as it promotes a South African–type apartheid: the "same water coming from different fountains" is not equal. As the American Supreme Court has decided "separate but equal" is not.

Tradition and change

6. *Because Christians realize that marriage has never been a static institution, and therefore there is no reason that it should be now.* From its early origin as a property exchange, to a method of ensuring peace between nations, to being recognized as a church function only in the thirteenth century, to the recent questioning of the "God-given" roles for men and women, the institution of marriage has always been in a state of flux. Things once illegal, such as miscegenation and the marriage of the mentally handicapped, are now permitted. To arbitrarily decide that now marriage has evolved as far as it should according to an 1960's definition is to deny any possible subsequent influence of the Holy Spirit in our world.

7. *Because Christians support the separation of Church and State.* Hardly anyone believes these days that the Church should define the law in this country—this position is ignorant of the centuries of problems that that historical situation created. In accordance with the freedom of religion in Canada, modern Christians realize that the insertion of the Christian God into government only spells trouble for those who (everyone agrees) have the right NOT to believe in that God. Christians do not want their denomination to dictate law for the rest of the country.

8. *Because Christians have long known that the Church should not determine legal policy.* Further to the above, Christians universally believe in following one's own conscience, even when that entails opposing the official policy of one's church. Catholics believe that each person has a solemn moral obligation to adhere to the dictates of his or her conscience (even if that conscience is erroneous), over and above the dictates of the Church. As Cardinal Ratzinger has written: "Only the absoluteness of conscience is the antithesis to tyranny." Thus for Catholics convicted that all Canadians should be treated equally and that the Canadian freedom of religion should be respected as above, not to promote the legalisation of same-sex marriages is sinful. Within Protestantism the case is even easier, as the entire tradition is ultimately based upon an individual acting according to the dictates of his conscience by nailing up 95 theses to the wall of a Wittenberg church, an act commemorated in most Protestant churches [at the end of each October]. To stand up and challenge the dominant authority is a practice firmly rooted and celebrated in Protestant tradition. Even those opposed to homosexuality in general can logically support same-sex marriage as a decidedly "lesser evil" than the alternative.

9. *Because Christians realize that to hold up marriage as for heterosexuals*

only is not only discriminatory, it also borders on idolatry. Just as the Pharisees in Jesus' day were maligned for counting their dill seeds while neglecting justice and mercy (Matthew 23:23), Christians today realize that marriage was created for humankind, not the opposite. Jesus' words in Mark 2:27 are an interesting parallel to the contemporary situation. Marriage is a tool for developing honest, voluntary, long-lasting and mutually accountable relationships between two people, and Christians realize that that is a laudable goal for two people of any gender and seek to promote that.

10. *Because Christians believe in the supremacy of God, not the supremacy of government.* Even those who consider homosexual behaviour to be sinful can believe in the equality of all people under the government. Christians realize that many sins are not covered by the Criminal Code, nor should they be, as they are more matters of individual conscience. Ultimately, Christians can take solace in the fact that all will be judged fairly before God, and leave it to God to do the judging. In the meantime, one can work toward the most equitable society possible on this earth: this is what Jesus would have us do.

The difficulty of defining "man" and "woman"

In yet another reason, educated Christians are also aware of the inherent difficulties in defining marriage as the exclusive union of one man and one woman: Olympic Committees and lawmakers alike realize the surprising impossibility of legally defining the terms "man" and "woman." True, for the majority of the population these things are self-evident, but a universal law applying to all Canadians must also take into account the 1 in 1,000 babies that are born intersexed (with anatomical, hormonal, or chromosomal differences that render them unable to conclusively determine a child's gender, let alone subsequent questions of orientation). The modern world is painfully beginning to realize that nature does not boil down into binary categories nearly as simply as we might like it to. The artificial dichotomy on sex and gender will be one of the final barriers to post-modern thinking to be lifted. If Christians are to seek justice in the world for all people this needs to include transgender individuals and intersexed people as well.

Instead of appearing reluctant or divided, the Christian Church should be among the leaders in taking a progressive and prophetic stance in this matter. By doing this not only would the Church be thus opening itself up to the moving of the Holy Spirit in the world, but this would also enable it to regain a sense of relevancy to contemporary society. It is only through supporting same-sex marriage that the Christian Church will be able to live up to its own standard of communicating the unconditional love of God and the radical inclusiveness of the Gospel of Jesus Christ to the entire world.

13

The Massachusetts Ruling Endorsing Gay Marriage Is Misguided

Stuart Taylor Jr.

Stuart Taylor Jr. is a senior writer and columnist for the National Journal *and a contributing editor at* Newsweek.

The 2003 gay marriage ruling in Massachusetts, which requires the state to allow gay unions, is misguided. Gay marriage is not an issue for the courts to decide. As a rule, court systems should always defer to laws enacted by legislative representatives who are chosen by voting citizens. The struggle for gay rights has made progress over the years, and that evolution will continue if it is pursued through the appropriate channels for a representative democracy. The Massachusetts Supreme Court decision, much like the similar "domestic partnership" decision in Vermont, prematurely forces the issue on the people of the United States and therefore will cause a backlash that ultimately will harm the goal of obtaining gay marriage rights.

A s a policy matter, gay marriage is an easy call. I'm for it. Many committed gay couples want very much to marry. A legislative vote giving them that right would cause no harm, except to psyches skewed by anti-gay animus—and those persons would remain free to express their moral disapproval. The arguments that gay marriage would damage traditional marriage by tempting people who might otherwise be straight and monogamous to become gay or promiscuous are extremely weak. So is the claim that gay marriage would be bad for children. Even assuming the much-disputed proposition that kids are better off in traditional than in gay households, legalizing gay marriage would not move any child out of a traditional household. Rather, it would bring the stability, respectability, and legal benefits of marriage to millions of children who are already being raised by gay and lesbian couples.

The constitutional question is much harder. The main reason is that a decent respect for government by the people should lead courts to defer to popularly enacted laws that embody deeply felt values—including laws that make no sense to the judges—unless the laws violate clear constitutional commands or fundamental rights. It is frivolous to claim that the marriage laws of every state and every civilization in the history of the world violate any clear constitutional command. And it is a stretch to claim that they flout fundamental rights.

The Massachusetts Supreme Judicial Court gave no deference to popular government in its November 18 [2003] decision, in a 4-3 vote, to legalize gay marriage. The court's wording suggests that it is prepared to go even to the point of ordering the state to call same-sex unions "marriage" rather than, say, "domestic partnerships" endowed with the same legal benefits.

Nor was there much prudence in this decision, which will take effect in May [2003]. The backlash it has provoked could conceivably prove powerful enough to set back the gay-rights movement for decades. In addition to energizing a push in Massachusetts to overrule the decision by amending the state constitution, the court has given new impetus to the proposed "Marriage Amendment" to the U.S. Constitution, a blunderbuss so broadly worded that it might block even state legislatures from legalizing gay marriage.

[In 2003], national polls showed a sudden drop in support for gay civil unions—from 49 percent in May to 37 percent in August.

Recent history suggests the power of the backlash. After the Hawaii Supreme Court and an Alaska court had signaled their intentions to legalize gay marriage, the citizens of both states overruled their courts in 1998, by 2-1 ratios amending their constitutions to ban same-sex marriage; 35 other states passed laws defining marriage as the union of a man and a woman; the federal Defense of Marriage Act decreed that federal law would not recognize any state's same-sex marriage and that no other state need recognize such a marriage. [In 2003], national polls showed a sudden drop in support for gay civil unions—from 49 percent in May to 37 percent in August—after the U.S. Supreme Court's June 26 decision in *Lawrence v. Texas*, which used unnecessarily grandiose language to strike down an oppressive Texas law criminalizing gay sex acts. And while gay marriage has more support in liberal Massachusetts than in most places, a national poll by the Pew Research Center [in October 2003] showed respondents opposing gay marriage by 59 to 32 percent.

Gay-marriage advocates have brought their cases under state constitutions because they fear that the U.S. Supreme Court would overturn any decision using the U.S. Constitution to legalize gay marriage. The justices have no jurisdiction to second-guess state courts' interpretations of their own constitutions.

Problems with the Massachusetts and Vermont rulings

In fairness to the Massachusetts court, its well-crafted opinion was a legally plausible extension of judicial precedents interpreting the Massachusetts

Constitution and the U.S. Constitution alike, especially *Lawrence*. But those precedents had already gone too far down the road of ramming judges' personal policy preferences down the throats of the voters, in the guise of constitutional interpretation.

Reasonable people disagree on this, of course, and decades of both conservative and liberal judicial activism have blurred the distinction between legitimate constitutional interpretation and illegitimate judicial fiat. These are not mutually exclusive categories, but points on either end of a continuum. The validity of any constitutional decision is a function of where it falls on that continuum—based on the plausibility of its derivation from the constitution's text, history, and structure—and whatever balance one strikes in resolving the dilemma identified by [U.S. federal court judge] Learned Hand in 1958:

> "Each one of us must in the end choose for himself how far he would like to leave our collective fate to the wayward vagaries of popular assemblies. . . ."

The Massachusetts court was certainly on firmer constitutional ground than its Vermont counterpart was in its 1999 gay-union decision, which it based on a completely irrelevant constitutional clause that had been adopted in 1777 for the apparent purpose of precluding creation of a legally privileged aristocracy. In a bold example of the "let's-do-it-because-we-can-get-away-with-it" school of jurisprudence, the Vermont court "interpreted" this clause as requiring recognition of either same-sex marriages or "domestic partnerships" with the same legal privileges. The state Legislature went for the "domestic partnership" compromise.

The Massachusetts court was hyperbolic to say that current marriage laws inflict "a deep and scarring hardship" on gays.

The Massachusetts court, on the other hand, based its ruling on Article I of the state constitution, whose provisions are roughly analogous to the 14th Amendment's due process and equal protection clauses. The first provision asserts: "All people are born free and equal and have certain natural, essential, and unalienable rights," including "the right of enjoying and defending their lives and liberties" and "that of seeking and obtaining their safety and happiness." The second provision states: "Equality of the law shall not be denied or abridged because of sex, race, color, creed, or national origin." Noting that "the two constitutional concepts . . . overlap," and are "more protective of individual liberty and equality" than the federal due process and equal protection clauses, the court held that Article I requires a right to gay marriage because the state's (very weak) justifications for denying it were "irrational."

While the Massachusetts court ignored (as usual) the original intent of Article I, it drew legal support from its own precedents, and moral support from *Lawrence*'s holding that voters' moral disapprobation of homosexuality is not a legitimate basis for legal distinctions that discriminate against gays and lesbians. The *Lawrence* decision "dismantled the structure of [federal] constitutional law that has permitted a distinction to be made between heterosexual and homosexual unions," as Justice Antonin Scalia wrote in dissent.

The courts overstretched their domain

So why do I think the Massachusetts court went too far? The first reason is that, in my view, *Lawrence* went too far. The majority's sweeping endorsement of "autonomy of self [in] intimate conduct" is well grounded in the moral philosophy of John Stuart Mill, but not in the language or history of the due process clause—the provision that the majority relied upon—or any other provision of the Constitution. The Court should have struck down the Texas sodomy statute on the narrower ground used by Justice Sandra Day O'Connor in her concurrence: By banning homosexual but not heterosexual sodomy, and thus singling out "one identifiable class of citizens for punishment that does not apply to everyone else," the Texas statute violated equal protection.

In addition, while withholding from gay couples what the Massachusetts court called the "tangible as well as intangible benefits [that] flow from marriage" is wrongheaded and unjust, it is simply not oppressive in the same sense as is criminalizing gay sexual intimacy. The Massachusetts court was hyperbolic to say that current marriage laws inflict "a deep and scarring hardship" on gays. It was arrogant to hold such laws "irrational," despite their deep roots in our history and popular values and in what dissenting Judge Robert Cordy called society's effort "to steer . . . acts of procreation and child-rearing into their most optimal setting." It was ahistorical to imply that gay marriage is a "fundamental right," a doctrine that would also require endorsement of polygamy and adult incest.

And while constitutional scholars have argued cogently in decades past for heightened judicial scrutiny of discrimination against gay people—a politically powerless minority long oppressed by majoritarian prejudice—gays now wield enough political clout to make such arguments somewhat anachronistic.

"The advancement of the rights, privileges, and protections afforded to homosexual members of our community in the last three decades has been significant," as Judge Cordy said, "and there is no reason to believe that the evolution will not continue." Unless the courts keep jumping the gun, and fueling the backlash.

14

Gay Families Are Gaining Greater Recognition

David Crary

David Crary is a writer for the Associated Press.

America's concept of the family is undergoing a significant shift as more nontraditional families are acknowledged. Gay and lesbian families are leading the way in gaining legal and cultural recognition. While some Americans still oppose the progress that has been made in same-sex family rights, many state and local governments, adoption agencies, and schools are moving toward welcoming gay and lesbian families. Most of the changes in policy toward nontraditional families have occurred case-by-case on the local or corporate level. As a result, comprehensive inclusion has been difficult to achieve.

William Carter's family doesn't fit the mold forged by early sitcoms or Dick-and-Jane storybooks, but the single gay man and his three adopted sons were honored . . . as the National Adoption Center's Family of the Year [in 2003].

Not an earth-shattering event, by itself, yet it epitomized a steady, profound change in Americans' concept of family—a development that some find heartening and others horrifying, but in any event seems to be quickening.

Changing the family concept

The traditional archetype of a mother, father and children still holds sway across much of America, though it now accounts for less than 25 percent of the nation's households. Many politicians, preachers and conservative activists envision that archetype when they speak in defense of "family values."

Yet ruling by ruling, vote by vote, in courtrooms and boardrooms and town halls nationwide, the makers of day-to-day policies are extending greater legal recognition and support to other forms of family—same-sex couples, unmarried heterosexual couples, single parents.

"Our families are becoming much more commonplace," said Aimee Gelnaw, who has raised two children with her lesbian partner and heads the Family Pride Coalition, a Washington-based advocacy group.

"Most people know someone who's lesbian or gay, in their communities, through their kids' schools," she said. "It's through those interactions that people come to understand we all want the same things—to create safe, loving environments for our kids."

Change alarms some: Debate over the American family is not new, but it has taken on extra intensity [in 2003] as the U.S. Supreme Court ruled that homosexual sex could not be outlawed and Canada moved to recognize same-sex marriages. Foes of same-sex marriage in the United States have been alarmed by the events.

"They didn't push me under the rug, they didn't talk down to me."

"Marriage at all times and in all civilizations has always meant the union of a man and a woman in a permanent relationship," said the Rev. Gerald Kieschnick, president of the 2.6-million member Lutheran Church–Missouri Synod. "To mess around with it is to threaten the very center of society—the family as it has been historically and universally understood."

Progress in gay family rights

Thirty-seven states have adopted Defense of Marriage Acts in recent years, defining marriage as a union between a man and a woman, and President [George W.] Bush said . . . he favors a law imposing that definition nationwide. Yet the state statutes and government initiatives to promote marriage have not slowed the growing acceptance and recognition of other types of families and relationships:

• Scores of cities, counties and corporations have adopted domestic-partner policies extending rights and benefits to same-sex couples and in some cases to unmarried heterosexual couples. The California Senate [considered] a sweeping bill, approved by the state Assembly, that would grant same-sex partners most of the same spousal rights and responsibilities as married couples.

• The New Mexico Supreme Court ruled in June [2003] that people in long-term relationships, married or not, can sue over loss of companionship when their loved one is injured. Lawyers say the ruling sets the groundwork for same-sex couples to file such claims.

• The supreme courts of Massachusetts and New Jersey [have taken] lawsuits filed by same-sex couples demanding the right to marry. The number of newspapers publishing announcements of same-sex unions has climbed past 200, more than triple the figure in 2001.

• Civil rights lawyers are pressing a federal lawsuit against a Florida law that prohibits adoptions by gays, the only one of its kind in the country. The Indiana Court of Appeals . . . ruled that a woman could adopt her lesbian partner's three children, rejecting a lower court ruling that the women could not both adopt because they aren't married.

A generation ago, adoptions by single people were rare. Now, about one-third of all adoptions in the United States are by single parents, and a growing number are men like Carter.

Gay and lesbian families

A property manager at a Philadelphia apartment complex, Carter has adopted three boys within the past three years, ages 10, 11 and 16.

"I always wanted to be a father," Carter said. "It's the best thing that's ever happened to me. . . . I would do anything for my boys."

He said he has received steady support from relatives, his employer and adoption agency staff.

"They didn't push me under the rug, they didn't talk down to me," he said. "The only advice they gave was that I shouldn't be looking for a perfect child, because there isn't one."

Gloria Hochman of the National Adoption Center said adoption agencies are gradually overcoming their hesitancies about single men because of the track record established by divorced fathers who, in growing numbers, are gaining custody of their children.

"When we opened our doors 30 years ago, it never occurred to me that we'd be giving our Family of the Year award to a single man," Hochman said. "We didn't think they'd be interested."

In South Orange, N.J., Fran Lipinski said she and her partner of 22 years, Melissa Hall, have been heartened by the community acceptance of their family, which since 1998 has included a daughter, Catherine, adopted from China.

When the two women were granted joint custody of Catherine, "it was a very upbeat ceremony," Lipinski recalled. "The judge came down off the bench to give us hugs."

Lipinski said the Family Pride Coalition sponsored a workshop for local school employees, and close to 100 teachers showed up for advice on how to make nontraditional families feel included in school activities.

Opposition to gay and lesbian families

To Jordan Lorence, a lawyer from Scottsdale, Ariz., such attitudes in public schools amount to indoctrination; he and his wife have decided to home school their six children.

"It's like a monastery in the Dark Ages that kept the biblical texts while everyone else was illiterate and falling apart," Lorence said. "The public schools are advocating a secularist, radical individualism, and we don't want our kids growing up with that."

Lorence is an attorney with the Alliance Defense Fund, which describes itself as a Christian legal organization seeking to defend religious freedom and traditional family values. Lorence is a critic of no-fault divorce, has waged legal fights against domestic-partner benefits and wrote a brief supporting the Texas sodomy law that was quashed by the Supreme Court.

"What we're going to have is sexual anarchy—all sorts of weird arrangements that are unimaginable, plural marriages, people coming together and breaking up quite easily with children being the victims of all this," he said.

Unmarried cohabitation is precisely the institution that Dorian Solot would like to defend. She and her partner of nine years, Marshall Miller, run the Boston-based Alternatives to Marriage Project and have written a guidebook for unwed couples, *Unmarried to Each Other*.

"People are far more comfortable with alternative families than they used to be," Solot said.

"On the other hand, the government is pouring money into promoting marriage," she added. "Politicians are afraid to say anything construed as antifamily. . . . They're worried they'll risk their careers if they talk about single parents or gay parents or unmarried couples."

Fighting for legitimacy

With only a handful of exceptions, most of the changes in policy toward nontraditional families have occurred piecemeal—at the local or corporate level—not through federal or state legislation.

"It's an ineffective way to effect change in family policies," said Barbara Risman, a sociology professor at North Carolina State University and co-chairwoman of the Council on Contemporary Families.

"Judges have no recourse but to make law on a case-by-case basis," she said. "It puts people at risk; families and couples can't protect themselves and their children in advance."

She said organizations that embrace the diversity of family forms need to work hard to be viewed as pro-family, not antifamily.

"The 'family values' groups—they only value a certain kind of family," Risman said. "Every kind of family has its challenges, and some families' challenges have to do with not being taken seriously as a family. They have to fight for legitimacy."

Organizations to Contact

The editors have compiled the following list of organizations concerned with the issues debated in this book. The descriptions are derived from materials provided by the organizations. All have publications or information available for interested readers. The list was compiled on the date of publication of the present volume; names, addresses, phone and fax numbers, and e-mail and Internet addresses may change. Be aware that many organizations take several weeks or longer to respond to inquiries, so allow as much time as possible.

Alliance for Marriage (AFM)
PO Box 2490, Merrifield, VA 22116
Web site: www.allianceformarriage.org

AFM is a nonprofit organization dedicated to promoting traditional marriage and addressing fatherless families in the United States. AFM works to prevent gay marriage and to educate the public, the media, elected officials, and civil leaders on the benefits of heterosexual marriage for children, adults, and society.

Alternative Family Matters
PO Box 390618, Cambridge, MA 02139
(617) 576-6788
Web site: www.alternativefamilies.org

Alternative Family Matters is an agency that assists lesbians, gay men, bisexuals, and transgendered people (LGBTs) who want to have children through artificial insemination, surrogacy, or adoption. The agency also educates the medical community to better understand and serve LGBT-headed families.

American Civil Liberties Union (ACLU) Lesbian and Gay Rights Project
125 Broad St., New York, NY 10004
(212) 549-2627
Web site: www.aclu.org

The ACLU is the nation's oldest and largest civil liberties organization. Its Lesbian and Gay Rights Project, started in 1986, handles litigation, education, and public-policy work on behalf of gays and lesbians. The union supports same-sex marriage. It publishes the monthly newsletter *Civil Liberties Alert*, the handbook *The Rights of Lesbians and Gay Men*, the briefing paper "Lesbian and Gay Rights," and the books *The Rights of Families: The ACLU Guide to the Rights of Today's Family Members* and *Making Schools Safe: An Anti-Harassment Training Program for Schools*.

Canadian Lesbian and Gay Archives
Box 639, Station A, Toronto, ON M5W 1G2 Canada
(416) 777-2755
Web site: www.clga.ca

The archives collects and maintains information and materials relating to the gay and lesbian rights movement in Canada and elsewhere. Its collection of records and other materials documenting the stories of lesbians and gay men and their organizations in Canada is available to the public for the purpose of education and research. It has published numerous books and pamphlets and publishes an annual newsletter, *Lesbian and Gay Archivist.*

Children of Lesbians and Gays Everywhere (COLAGE)
3543 Eighteenth St. #1, San Francisco, CA 94110
(415) 861-KIDS (5437) • fax: (415) 255-8345
Web site: www.colage.org

COLAGE is an international organization to support young people with gay, lesbian, bisexual, or transgendered parents. It coordinates pen pal and scholarship programs, and sponsors an annual Family Week to celebrate family diversity. COLAGE publishes a quarterly newsletter and maintains several e-mail discussion lists.

Concerned Women for America (CWA)
1015 Fifteenth St. NW, Suite 1100, Washington, DC 20005
(202) 488-7000 • fax: (202) 488-0806
Web site: www.cwfa.org

CWA is an educational and legal defense foundation that seeks to strengthen the traditional family by applying Judeo-Christian moral standards. It opposes gay marriage and the granting of additional civil rights protections to gays and lesbians. It publishes the monthly magazine *Family Voice* and various position papers on gay marriage and other issues.

Eagle Forum
PO Box 618, Alton, IL 62002
(618) 462-5415 • fax: (618) 462-8909
Web site: www.eagleforum.org

A political action group, Eagle Forum advocates traditional, biblical values. It believes mothers should stay home with their children, and it favors policies that support the traditional family and reduce government involvement in family issues. The forum opposes an equal rights amendment and gay rights legislation. It publishes the monthly *Phyllis Schlafly Report* and *Education Reporter.*

Family Pride Coalition
PO Box 65327, Washington, DC 20035
(202) 331-5015 • fax: (202) 331-0080
Web site: www.familypride.org

The coalition advocates for the well-being of lesbian, gay, bisexual, and transgendered (LGBT) parents and their families through mutual support, community collaboration, and public understanding. It lobbies for positive public policy, educates communities about LGBT families, and provides information for LGBT families to enhance their lives. Family Pride publishes numerous pamphlets such as *How to Talk to Children About Our Families*, and the quarterly newsletter *Family Tree.*

Family Research Institute (FRI)
PO Box 62640, Colorado Springs, CO 80962
(303) 681-3113
Web site: www.familyresearchinst.org

The FRI distributes information about family, sexual, and substance abuse issues. The institute believes that strengthening traditional marriage would reduce many social problems, including crime, poverty, and sexually transmitted diseases. The FRI publishes the monthly newsletter *Family Research Report* as well as the pamphlets *Same-Sex Marriage: Til Death Do Us Part??* and *Homosexual Parents: A Comparative Study*.

Focus on the Family
8685 Explorer Dr., Colorado Springs, CO 80920
(719) 531-3400 • (800) 232-6459
Web site: www.family.org

Focus on the Family is a Christian organization that seeks to strengthen the traditional family in America. It believes the family is the most important social unit and maintains that reestablishing the traditional two-parent family will end many social problems. In addition to conducting research and educational programs, Focus on the Family publishes the monthly periodicals *Focus on the Family* and *Citizen* as well as the reports *Setting the Record Straight: What Research Really Says About the Consequences of Homosexuality* and *Twice as Strong: The Undeniable Advantages of Raising Children in a Traditional Two-Parent Family*.

Howard Center for Family, Religion, and Society
934 N. Main St., Rockford, IL 61103
(815) 964-5819 • fax: (815) 965-1826
Web site: www.profam.org

The Howard Center conducts research to affirm the traditional family and religion as the foundation of a free and virtuous society. The organization operates the John L. Swan Library on Family and Culture, a large collection of conservative family literature. The center publishes the monthly periodicals *Family in America* and *Religion and Society Report* and the supplemental *New Research* newsletter.

Human Rights Campaign FamilyNet (HRC FamilyNet)
1640 Rhode Island Ave. NW, Washington, DC 20036
(202) 628-4160
Web site: www.hrc.org

HRC FamilyNet is a clearinghouse of information for lesbian, gay, bisexual, and transgendered families coordinated by the Human Rights Campaign Foundation. It provides information and resources about adoption, civil unions, coming out, custody and visitation, donor insemination, family law, families of origin, marriage, money, parenting, religion, schools, senior health and housing, state laws and legislation, straight spouses, and transgender and workplace issues. FamilyNet publishes numerous reports and the biweekly *HRC FamilyNet News*.

Lambda Legal Defense and Education Fund
120 Wall St., Suite 1500, New York, NY 10005
(212) 809-8585 • fax: (212) 809-0055
Web site: www.lambdalegal.org

Lambda is a public interest law firm committed to achieving full recognition of the civil rights of lesbians, gay men, and people with HIV/AIDS. The firm addresses a variety of topics, including equal marriage rights, parenting and relationship issues, and domestic-partner benefits. It believes marriage is a basic right and an individual choice. Lambda publishes the quarterly *Lambda Update*, the pamphlet *Freedom to Marry*, and several position papers on same-sex marriage and gay and lesbian family rights.

National Center for Lesbian Rights (NCLR)
870 Market St., Suite 570, San Francisco, CA 94102
(415) 392-8442
Web site: www.nclrights.org

The center is a public interest law office that provides legal counseling and representation to victims of sexual-orientation discrimination. Primary areas of advice include child custody and parenting, employment, housing, the military, and insurance. Among the center's publications are the pamphlets *Same-Sex Relationship Recognition* and *Adoption by Lesbian, Gay, Bisexual, and Transgender Parents: An Overview of the Current Law*.

National Gay and Lesbian Task Force (NGLTF)
1325 Massachusetts Ave. NW, Suite 600, Washington, DC 20005
(202) 393-5177 • fax: (202) 393-2241
Web site: www.ngltf.org

The NGLTF is a civil rights advocacy organization that lobbies Congress and the White House on a range of civil rights and AIDS issues affecting gays and lesbians. The organization is working to make same-sex marriage legal. It publishes numerous papers and pamphlets, the booklets *Family Policy: Issues Affecting Gay, Lesbian, Bisexual and Transgender Families* and *Massachusetts Equal Marriage Rights Policy Brief*, and the quarterly *The Task Force Report*.

Parents, Families, and Friends of Lesbians and Gays (PFLAG)
1726 M St. NW, Suite 400, Washington, DC 20036
(202) 467-8180 • fax: (202) 467-8194
Web site: www.pflag.org

PFLAG is a national organization that provides support and education services for gays, lesbians, bisexuals, and their families and friends. It also works to end prejudice and discrimination against homosexuals. It publishes and distributes pamphlets and articles, including *Faith in Our Families, Our Daughters and Sons: Questions and Answers for Parents of Gay, Lesbian, Bisexual, and Transgendered People*, and *Hate Crimes Hurt Families*.

Traditional Values Coalition (TVC)
139 C St. SE, Washington, DC 20003
(202) 547-8570 • fax: (202) 546-6403
Web site: www.traditionalvalues.org

The coalition strives to restore what the group believes are the traditional moral and spiritual values in American government, schools, media, and society. It believes that gay marriage threatens the family unit and extends civil rights beyond what the coalition considers appropriate limits. The coalition publishes the newsletter *TVC Weekly News* as well as various information papers addressing same-sex marriage and other issues.

Bibliography

Books

Jack O. Balswick, Judith K. Balswick, and Judy Balswick
The Family: A Christian Perspective on the Contemporary Home. Grand Rapids, MI: Baker Book House, 1999.

Nijole V. Benokraitus
Feuds About Families: Conservative, Centrist, Liberal, and Feminist Perspectives. New York: Prentice-Hall, 1999.

Robert A. Bernstein, Betty DeGeneres, and Robert MacNeil
Straight Parents, Gay Children: Keeping Families Together. New York: Thunder's Mouth, 2003.

Stephanie A. Brill
The Queer Parent's Primer: A Lesbian and Gay Families' Guide to Navigating the Straight World. Oakland, CA: New Harbinger, 2001.

Christopher Carrington
No Place Like Home: Relationships and Family Life Among Lesbians and Gay Men. Chicago: University of Chicago Press, 1999.

D. Merilee Clunis and G. Dorsey Green
The Lesbian Parenting Book: A Guide to Creating Families and Raising Children. Seattle: Seal, 2003.

William N. Eskridge and William N. Eskridge Jr.
Equality Practice: Civil Unions and the Future of Gay Rights. New York: Routledge, 2001.

Abigail Garner
Families Like Mine: Children of Gay Parents Tell It Like It Is. New York: HarperCollins, 2004.

Evan Gerstmann
Same-Sex Marriage and the Constitution. New York: Cambridge University Press, 2003.

Andrew R. Gottlieb
Out of the Twilight: Fathers of Gay Men Speak. New York: Haworth, 2000.

Andrew R. Gottlieb
Sons Talk About Their Gay Fathers: Life's Curves. New York: Harrington Park, 2003.

Lynn Haley-Banez and Joanne Garrett
Lesbians in Committed Relationships: Extraordinary Couples, Ordinary Lives. New York: Harrington Park, 2002.

Hendrik Hartog
Man and Wife in America: A History. Cambridge, MA: Harvard University Press, 2002.

Daniel A. Helminiak
What the Bible Really Says About Homosexuality. San Francisco: Alamo Square, 2000.

Janet R. Jakobsen and Ann Pellegrini
Love the Sin: Sexual Regulation and the Limits of Tolerance. Boston: Beacon, 2004.

105

Stephen Macedo and Iris Marion Young	*Child, Family, and State.* New York: New York University Press, 2003.
Gerald P. Mallon	*Gay Men Choosing Parenthood.* New York: Columbia University Press, 2004.
David Moats	*Civil Wars: Gay Marriage in America.* New York: Harcourt, 2004.
Joseph Nicolosi and Linda Ames Nicolosi	*A Parent's Guide to Preventing Homosexuality.* Downers Grove, IL: InterVarsity, 2002.
Ralph R. Smith and Russel R. Windes	*Progay/Antigay: The Rhetorical War over Sexuality.* Thousand Oaks, CA: Sage, 2000.
Judith E. Snow	*How It Feels to Have a Lesbian or Gay Parent: A Book by Kids for Kids of All Ages.* New York: Harrington Park, 2004.
Gretchen A. Stiers	*From This Day Forward: Commitment, Marriage, and Family in Lesbian and Gay Relationships.* New York: Palgrave Macmillan, 2000.
John R.W. Stott	*Same-Sex Partnerships?: A Christian Perspective.* New York: Fleming H. Revell, 1998.
David Strah and Susanna Margolis	*Gay Dads: A Celebration of Fatherhood.* Los Angeles: J.P. Tarcher, 2003.
Linda Waite and Maggie Gallagher	*The Case for Marriage: Why Married People Are Happier, Healthier, and Better Off Financially.* Louisville, KY: Broadway, 2001.
Jeffrey Weeks, Brian Heaphy, and Catherine Donovan	*Same-Sex Intimacies: Families of Choice and Other Life Experiments.* New York: Routledge, 2001.

Periodicals

Advocate	"Our Readers Get Married," February 17, 2004.
Joshua K. Baker	"Summary of Opinion Research on Same-Sex Marriage," *iMAPP Policy Brief,* December 5, 2003.
Ginia Bellafante	"Two Fathers, with One Happy to Stay Home," *New York Times,* January 12, 2004.
Karen Breslau et al.	"Outlaw Vows," *Newsweek,* March 1, 2004.
Chris Bull	"What Makes a Mom," *Advocate,* November 25, 2003.
Christianity Today	"Let No Law Put Asunder," February 2004.
Victoria Clarke	"What About the Children? Arguments Against Lesbian and Gay Parenting," *Women's Studies International Forum,* September/October 2001.
Lynette Clemetson	"Both Sides Court Black Churches in the Battle over Gay Marriage," *New York Times,* March 1, 2004.
CQ Researcher	"Disputed Studies Give Gay Parents Good Marks," September 5, 2003.

Lisa Duggan	"Holy Matrimony!" *Nation*, March 15, 2004.
Economist	"Out in Front," February 21, 2004.
Franklin Foer	"Marriage Counselor," *Atlantic Monthly*, March 2004.
Dan Gilgoff et al.	"Tied in Knots by Gay Marriage," *U.S. News & World Report*, March 8, 2004.
Erica Goode	"A Rainbow of Differences in Gays' Children," *New York Times*, July 17, 2001.
Linda Harvey	"The World According to PFLAG: Why PFLAG and Children Don't Mix," *National Association for Research and Therapy of Homosexuality*, December 2002.
John W. Kennedy	"Gay Parenting on Trial," *Christianity Today*, July 8, 2002.
Stanley Kurtz	"Oh Canada! Will Gay Marriage Stand?" *National Review*, June 13, 2003.
Richard Lacayo	"For Better or for Worse?" *Time*, February 29, 2004.
Rona Marech	"Devastating Side of Gay Liberation: Straight Spouse Network Eases Pain," *San Francisco Chronicle*, January 6, 2003.
Michael McAuliffe	"Love and the Law," *National*, May 19, 1999.
National Review	"The Right Amendment," January 26, 2004.
George Neumayr	"Marriage on the Rocks," *American Spectator*, February 2004.
Newsweek	"The War over Gay Marriage," July 7, 2003.
Dennis O'Brien	"A More Perfect Union," *Christian Century*, January 27, 2004.
John O'Sullivan	"The Bells Are Ringing . . . ," *National Review*, March 8, 2004.
Katha Pollitt	"Adam and Steve: Together at Last," *Nation*, December 15, 2003.
Scott Sherman	"Our Son Is Happy, What Else Matters?" *Newsweek*, September 16, 2002.
Andrew Sullivan	"Why the M Word Matters to Me," *Time*, February 16, 2004.
Chris Taylor	"I Do . . . No You Don't!" *Time*, March 1, 2004.
Jyoti Thottam	"Why Breaking Up Is So Hard to Do," *Time*, March 1, 2004.
USA Today Magazine	"Adoption More Open for Gays and Lesbians," April 2003.
David Usborne	"Gay with Children," *New York*, November 3, 2003.
Jacqueline Woodson	"Motherhood, My Way," *Essence*, December 2003.

Index